CHINA'S 90% MODEL

Other Books by Ram Charan

1. Action, Urgency, Excellence
2. Boards at Work
3. Boards That Deliver
4. Boards That Lead (co-author)
5. Business Acumen (customized book for Ford Motor Company)
6. Confronting Reality (co-author)
7. Digital Simplified (co-author)
8. E-Board Strategies (co-author)
9. Every Business Is a Growth Business
10. Execution (co-author)
11. Getting Things Done
12. Global Tilt
13. Harsh Realities (co-author)
14. Know-How
15. Leaders at All Levels
16. Leading Through Inflation
17. Leadership in the Era of Economic Uncertainty
18. n=1: How the Uniqueness of Each Individual Is Transforming Healthcare (co-author)
19. Owning Up
20. Profitable Growth Is Everyone's Business
21. Rethinking Competitive Advantage (co-author)
22. Solid Line, Dotted Line, Bottom Line (customized book for Gateway)
23. Strategic Management: A Casebook in Business Policy and Planning (co-author)
24. Talent Wins (co-author)
25. Talent, Strategy, Risk (co-author)
26. Talent: The Market Cap Multiplier (co-author)
27. The Amazon Management System (co-author)
28. The Attacker's Advantage
29. The Digital Leader (co-author)
30. The Game-Changer (co-author)
31. The High Potential Leader
32. The Leadership Pipeline (co-author)
33. The Phoenix Encounter Method (co-author)
34. The Talent Masters (co-author)
35. Verizon Untethered (co-author)
36. What the CEO Wants You to Know
37. What the Customer Wants You to Know

CHINA'S 90% MODEL

China Has America by the Throat
Here's How to Fight Back and WIN

RAM CHARAN

Co-Author of the #1 NEW YORK TIMES Bestseller EXECUTION

WASHINGTON, D.C.

Ideapress Publishing | www.ideapresspublishing.com

Cover + Interior Design: Jessica Angerstein

Cataloging-in-Publication Data is on file with the Library of Congress.

Hardcover ISBN: 978-1-64687-245-9

Special Sales
Ideapress books are available at a special discount for bulk purchases for sales promotions and premiums, or for use in corporate training programs. Special editions, including personalized covers, a custom foreword, corporate imprints, and bonus content, are also available.

1 2 3 4 5 6 7 8 9 10

Dedicated to the hearts and souls of the joint family of twelve siblings and cousins living under one roof for fifty years, whose personal sacrifices made my formal education possible.

—Ram Charan

CONTENTS

The Wake-Up Call

On Friday, October 10, 2025, something extraordinary happened. A declaration by China that would shake the world. And it went largely unnoticed.

President Xi Jinping announced that Chinese exporters would require licenses to export specific items—items that could shut down entire industries in America and other targeted countries at will.[1] The pace of that shutdown, the magnitude of the damage, would depend entirely on how Beijing chose to exercise that choke hold.

This was not a bluff. China had already imposed restrictions on magnet exports, forcing President Trump to retaliate with additional tariffs. But this October statement was different. It was a declaration. A line crossed. A lethal weapon more powerful than any military arsenal—operable within one week, with no shots fired, no loss of life, but capable of stopping entire sectors of the economy in their tracks. Instant unemployment. Total disruption. National security at risk.

Trump's response was immediate and severe: 100 percent tariffs on all Chinese exports.[2] The chairman of the House Select Committee on China announced what many still refuse to accept: **The United States (US) and China are now actively at war.**

Not a cold war. Not a trade dispute. A war. Economic, technological, and increasingly, existential. **A war of mutual destruction.**

Most people still don't see it. The press doesn't understand the gravity of Xi controlling the world's economies at will. The public doesn't realize that anything they buy today can be blocked by Xi tomorrow. But if you run a company, sit on a board, or manage a supply chain, you are already in the line of fire. Either directly, or indirectly through extended supply chain.

This is more than an economic war. It is **total preparation for military conflict**. Proxy wars are already being fought—Russia in Ukraine, with China's full backing. And it is spilling into the political sphere as China works to pull countries out of America's orbit and into its own.

This is the US-China War. And there is no end in sight.

The war has already begun. Factories are the new front lines. Currency is the new artillery. Data is the new terrain.

The march accelerates. In November 2025, Trump announced plans to resume nuclear weapons testing.[3] America is allocating resources to readiness that it will never recover for other national priorities. Meanwhile, watch India: forced to settle Russian oil purchases in yuan[4] to bypass sanctions, yet simultaneously pressured[5] by Washington to reduce those same Russian oil purchases. This is what the contest looks like on the ground—every player squeezed, forced to navigate **impossible contradictions**, choosing sides in real-time.

If you are just now **waking up** to this reality, you are late. But you are not too late.

THE BRILLIANCE OF PRESIDENT XI'S STRATEGY

I have spent 60 years advising the world's largest corporations—Intel, Honeywell, GE, Pfizer, and over 200 others across America, Brazil, China, Japan, and beyond. I hold a doctorate in corporate governance and taught at Harvard Business School. I have advised roughly 100 boards and written over 36 books. I have been advising in China for more than 30 years, working with over 50 companies there, coaching many high-profile CEOs, and serving on the boards of Chinese companies.

My engagements with these companies have never lasted less than 10 years. Many have extended 40 years. Why? Because I do not propose theories. I propose **actions my clients can execute. Actions that work.**

I started writing this book five years ago.

Let me be clear: **Every CEO doing business in China is in awe of President Xi's brilliant strategy**. The high quality. The low prices. The high productivity. The coordination. The execution.

Give credit where it is due: This strategy was **invisible** because it was **insidious.** Only those whose supply chains were destroyed, whose prices were trashed, or who were forced into joint ventures felt the pain early. Everyone else—consumers, retailers, CEOs, Wall Street—saw only benefits. Lower costs. Better margins. Higher returns. Who would complain?

Since becoming general secretary of the Chinese Communist Party in 2012, Xi has executed a strategy so meticulous, so coordinated, and so effective that it has reshaped the global order. He has encircled America economically, technologically, militarily, and now through logistics and data flows. He has systematically dismantled American industrial capacity while building China's into an unstoppable machine.

Put yourself in President Xi's shoes, and you will see the brilliance. Underestimating Xi is a delusion.

THE HIDDEN WAR: THE 90 PERCENT MODEL

Here is what most people do not understand: **China's economic model is designed to destroy competitors**, not just outcompete them.

At the heart of all this is what I call the 90 Percent Excess Production Capacity Model. And people have not understood it.

China's strategy is brutally simple:

Build enough industrial capacity to meet 90 percent of global demand in a targeted sector. Undervalue the currency by about 20 percent to make exports unbeatable on price. Flood the market with subsidized exports priced at or below marginal cost. Force competitors out of business. Dominate the sector. Then move to the next one.

China has already done this in apparel, furniture, toys, and solar panels. Now it is targeting the industries that matter most: automobiles, defense, semiconductors, critical minerals, pharmaceuticals, chemicals, telecom, and others. Industries that are not just economically critical but **strategically vital to national security**.

And here is what should shake every policymaker and CEO: **Almost all of this high-quality, high-tech manufacturing in China has been built in the last 10 years**. All of it is funded by trade surpluses accumulated through currency manipulation. And the know-how? It came from America and its allies.

And here is the part that should **terrify** every CEO and policymaker: China can now shut down entire industries in other countries **at will**.

Take the chemical industry. It has reached a point where large segments in Europe and America are suffering, and plants are being closed. American companies are finding niche customers just to survive. It is under the radar. The press does not know it. The public does not either. Olin shut major US chlorine and chemical plants,[6] citing high costs and overseas competition. BASF shuttered ammonia units and sold off high-value pigment divisions.[7] In Europe, LyondellBasell and Tronox have closed Rotterdam plants, blaming Chinese overcapacity.[8]

The magnet restrictions were just the beginning. In October 2025, Xi made it explicit: China controls the choke points. Rare earths. Battery components. Advanced chemicals. Semiconductor materials. If Beijing decides to cut off supply, industries in the United States, Europe, Japan, and South Korea grind to a halt.

This is power. **Asymmetric power.** And Xi has built it step-by-step.

December 2025: China's global trade surplus reached $1.08 trillion in just 11 months.[9] A record no country in history has ever achieved. President Trump's most aggressive tariffs were not enough to slow the export flood.

The hard cash keeps flowing from America and its allies to China. And China keeps converting it into a military and industrial machine encircling the free world.

This is the culmination of decades of **systematic exploitation.**

THE RIGGED SYSTEM

But Xi did not build this in isolation. **The global trading system has been rigged for decades**, and almost no one noticed until it was too late.

Nearly every major trading partner developed rigid systems to exclude imports while flooding the US market. Japan. South Korea. Germany. China. They subsidize exporters, block consumer and agricultural imports, and manipulate currencies to stay artificially cheap. This is not accident. It is strategy. They accumulate reserves. They protect industries. They prosper at America's expense.

The US is the world's largest consumer market, growing at 3 percent annually.[10] Every country wants access. But they do not reciprocate. They trade for market access, not fair exchange.

The pattern is clear across history: **Countries that strengthen their currency climb to first-world status.** Why? Strong currency lets them import technology, equipment, and know-how. That builds first-world economies.

The Singapore dollar appreciated from roughly 3 to 1.35 against the dollar over the past five decades.[11] Painful at first. But the stronger currency forced Singapore up the value chain, allowed it to import better technology, and turned it into a high-value exporter. Taiwan and South Korea followed similar paths—strengthening currencies and climbing to first-world status through discipline.

China did the opposite. It depreciated 52 percent since 1990,[12] layered extreme subsidies, absorbed massive losses, and—through political control enforced by fear—powered itself into the world's second-largest economy. Command economics that the world failed to detect.

This is the system that must now be dismantled. The path forward requires a doctrine America has never formally adopted: **zero balance of trade over a manageable period.** Not protectionism. Partnership. You want access to the world's largest market? Fine. The trade must flow both ways. **Bilateral zero balance.**

HOW WE GOT HERE

For decades, American leaders assumed that economic integration would make China a responsible stakeholder in the global system. That trade would soften authoritarianism. That openness would win.

They were wrong. And they were naive. And they failed to bring anyone else along. Washington did a **miserable job bringing constituencies on board**. No systematic explanation of China's 90 Percent Model to the public, to business leaders, to the press. Political experts miss the systematic encirclement. Even diplomats who should know better often don't. That silence let Xi's strategy advance unchallenged.

China took everything the West offered—technology, capital, market access—and used it to build a system designed to replace the American-led world order. Not reform it. Replace it.

American leaders, all leaders other than Trump, hesitated to take the actions needed. They feared a war of global proportions. **Without cogent ally coordination, one cannot stop the march of President Xi.**

President Trump, in his first term, sounded the alarm. He imposed tariffs. He recognized the threat. But his approach was unilateral, chaotic, and lacked the coordination needed to counter a strategy as comprehensive as Xi's.

President Biden continued some of Trump's policies but wrapped them in softer language: "de-risking," "friend-shoring," "small yard, high fence." The intent was right. The execution was insufficient.

Now, in Trump's second term, the approach has sharpened. Tariffs are higher. Restrictions are tighter. The rhetoric is more aggressive. Trump has discovered what I have been saying for years: **Tariffs alone will not work.**

Why? Because unless you address the root cause, **currency manipulation**, China will always have an advantage. **China's deliberate 52 percent currency devaluation**—from 4.8 renminbi (RMB) per dollar in 1990 to 7.3 in 2024—is how Chinese exports remain artificially cheap. That is how China sustains its trade surplus. That is how it funds its military expansion, its Belt and Road Initiative, and its technological ambitions.

Tariffs can slow China down. But they **cannot stop the march unless they are combined with** currency realignment, allied coordination, industrial rebuilding at hyperscale, blocking China's path to markets, and deploying financial weapons to destroy the Beijing economic model.

TRUMP'S RUDE AWAKENING

Something fundamental has shifted. President Trump is shocked. He feels deceived by both President Xi and Vladimir Putin.

He now knows there is no trust. Not with Xi. Not with Putin. Not with Kim Jong Un in North Korea. The illusion that personal rapport could soften authoritarians has been shattered. Personal diplomacy fails with autocrats. The evidence is conclusive.

To his credit, Trump is quick to shift, improvise, and learn. He has done this all his life. But this creates chaos and panic for business leaders trying to plan in an environment where the rules change weekly.

And here is what Trump has discovered that changes everything: The war in Ukraine is not just Russia's war. It is China's war, fought through a proxy. Every dollar, every sanction, every weapon system diverted to Ukraine is one less focused on China. That is Beijing's strategy. **Distraction. Attrition. Fragmentation.**

Trump has also discovered that China's choke hold on critical materials—magnets, rare earths, semiconductors, pharmaceuticals—gives Beijing leverage that tariffs alone cannot break.

I believe Trump is on the right track. He must persist to knock down the 90 Percent Model. But he needs to ensure that excess inventory does not simply shift to other markets. And he needs allies. Committed collaboration now is urgent.

Trump's past approach was containment. Fighting China from a position of weakness. Pure tit-for-tat: tariff for tariff, restriction for restriction. But in that game, China holds the advantage today. They have the choke points. They have the capacity. They can outlast us in a straight fight.

The shift must be toward coexistence—not surrender, but calculated pragmatism. Give China something they value in exchange for what America needs more: time to rebuild, currency adjustments that stick, and the breathing room to coordinate with allies.

This is not about trusting China. This is about buying the three to five years needed to knock down the 90 Percent Model, force currency realignment, rebuild industrial capacity with allies, and race ahead on next-generation technology.

Coexistence in some domains. Dominance in the ones that matter. And time, bought through smart negotiation, to execute convergence with allies.

THE THRESHOLD OF PAIN

So here is what I predict: In 2026, President Trump will change his approach toward allies.

Why? Because he now understands what I have been arguing in boardrooms and policy circles for years: **America cannot win this fight alone.**

Beijing will not stop unless it feels pain. The only language it respects is consequence. When two opponents compete, each must assess the other's threshold, the point beyond which behavior changes. America must continuously monitor Xi's moves, predict his responses, and deploy every tool to reach that threshold: tariffs, export controls, financial pressure, and allied coordination. **Whatever it takes.**

Game theorist John Nash won the Nobel Prize for demonstrating how rational actors reach equilibrium through strategic interdependence.[13] Xi will not change course until continuing costs more than adjusting.

I was in a meeting recently with a senior Washington official and CEOs. His assessment was stark: *"America has never faced an adversary like this. Russia, Iran, China—all connected. They have infiltrated our institutions at hyperscale. The goal is a status quo relationship. But you cannot negotiate your way there. Only through the threshold of pain."*

That pain cannot come from America alone. It must come from a **coordinated bloc**—the United States, the European Union, Japan, South Korea, Israel, and the United Kingdom—an alliance commanding nearly **$60 trillion in GDP**.[14] Together, these six command more than twice China's sphere of roughly $25 trillion (Russia, Iran, Venezuela, North Korea, and their aligned states).[15] Between them lie 180 unaligned countries with another $25 trillion.[16] Most will choose the American Sphere over China's coercive model.

These six regions anchor the American Sphere. Taiwan, Canada, Australia, India, and others form a broader ecosystem. What matters is that the core six set the standards, coordinate the policies, and lead with clarity. Others will follow.

Not through containment. Not through decoupling. Through **convergence.**

Time has run out. Convergence must start now.

WHAT CONVERGENCE REALLY MEANS

Convergence is not a summit. It is not a declaration. **It is an operating system for the free world.**

It means the six-region bloc coordinates policies, aligns investments, and rebuilds industrial capacity together. It means currency realignment happens simultaneously across all surplus nations. It means supply chains are rewired, critical industries are rebuilt, and technology protection is enforced with the same discipline as military alliances.

It means synchronized tariffs, joint investments, shared supply-chain intelligence, and aligned currency policies. It means acting as a single economic front, as tightly bound as the North Atlantic Treaty Organization (NATO) is militarily.

This is what NATO and AUKUS (a security pact between the US, Australia, and the United Kingdom) have done for military coordination. Convergence must do the same for industrial coordination.

And here is why it will work: **China cannot compete with $60 trillion in coordinated GDP.** Not sustainably. Not over decades. Xi knows this. That is why he is working so hard to fracture the alliance before it forms.

But if the American Sphere comes together—if Trump shifts to multilateral coordination, if Europe stops hedging, if Japan and South Korea align fully, if the UK commits—China's advantage disappears.

That is convergence. And it is the only path forward.

REBUILDING THE ARSENAL

At the heart of convergence is a building block that may sound ambitious, but I believe we must do it: **creating a new Department of Manufacturing and Advanced Technology**. We have done this before. In World War II, the United States' rapid production of Liberty ships averaged 1.5 per day.[17] That level of industrial mobilization is what we need again.

Here is what gives me hope: **The people who built China's manufacturing capacity are still alive. And they are available.** Most of them are in the West. I know Americans who, in the case of Apple, slept on factory floors in China training workers to manufacture precision components. They did it once. They can do it again.

The Chinese people have told me how grateful they are to the United States. But they are under the control of a party that is imposing its will not just in China, but on the US and beyond.

The will of the administration should be to find these people and focus on them to trigger a manufacturing renaissance. Americans who trained China's workers. Engineers who designed the systems. Supply-chain architects who made it all work.

Make equity available. JPMorgan Chase has already pledged $10 billion for "America First" investments in US companies critical to national security and economic resilience, as part of a broader $1.5 trillion commitment.[18] That capital is ready. The expertise exists. What is missing is coordination and urgency.

That coordination requires a national war room. Not bureaucracy, but a command center operating at crisis speed—recruiting elite talent, modeling China's moves in real time using AI, feeding decisions directly to the president and cabinet. It must transcend presidential terms and stay bipartisan. Every ally in the American Sphere must mirror this structure. Together, these war rooms coordinate investments, align standards, and share intelligence on supply chains and security threats. Speed is now a strategic advantage.

Our people can do a lot within three to five years. **Year One:** establish Department of Manufacturing and Advanced Technology, align tariffs, begin currency realignment, launch pilot investments. **Years Two–Three:** scale manufacturing buildout, diversify supply chains, train workforce. **Years Four–Five:** complete transition, achieve independence from Chinese choke points.

And after six months of starting, the **psychology will shift**. Energy will return. When people see factories opening, jobs being created, supply chains rewiring—they will believe again.

That belief is a weapon. It changes investor confidence. It changes worker morale. It changes allied commitment. And it terrifies Beijing.

THE PRICE OF SURVIVAL

Let me be honest about what this will cost.

Prices will go up in key industries such as defense, semiconductors, telecom, chemicals, and automobiles. But fears of inflation are overblown. These sectors and their supply chains represent around 15 percent of GDP.[19] In most cases, Chinese inputs are a small fraction of the total unit cost. Cost-cutting has already begun. Companies will absorb what they can and pass through the rest.

The JPMorgan money and other investments are flowing into industries critical to national security. People have to understand that **higher prices in some sectors are the cost of resilience**. Industries like services—the biggest contributor to GDP—are locally driven, so they are not dependent on global geopolitics.

This is not a recession. This is an investment in survival. And those who complete the transition will have lower geopolitical risk, more control over their destiny, and long-term competitive advantage.

Meanwhile, President Trump's tax cuts, pressure on interest rates, and incoming investments are drivers of economic growth that will offset any transitional pain. The **Commerce Department's Investment Accelerator is fast-tracking projects over $1 billion**, slashing regulatory delays.[20]

Nearly $9 trillion[21] in new investments have been announced as of late 2025. Nvidia, SoftBank, OpenAI's Stargate, Apple, and sovereign funds from the UAE, Qatar, and Japan are flooding capital into US operations.

THE CRITICAL PERIOD AHEAD

The intensity of this contest is accelerating. By the time you read this, we will likely have witnessed further escalation. Trump ratcheting up pressure. Xi deploying new export controls. Action. Reaction. Action again.

This **tit-for-tat escalation** will not stop. It will intensify throughout 2026 and beyond.

And here is the danger: Miscommunication. Miscalculation. One move that pushes both sides to the brink of something far more dangerous than an economic war.

Clouds of war preparation are gathering all over the world. In every country, exercises and simulations are underway. Defense expenditures are increasing because they expect something could happen. That is robbing economic growth and innovation.

We are operating in what *The Wall Street Journal* calls *"combustible geopolitics"*—a world where every trade flow, every alliance shift, every tariff announcement can ignite broader conflict.

The Russia-Ukraine war shows no sign of ending. It has been nearly four years, and Xi's support for Putin ensures it continues. In November 2025, Xi met Russian Prime Minister Mishustin in Beijing, pledging expanded investment in energy, agriculture, aerospace, and digital technology.[22] While Western sanctions tighten, Xi deepens the partnership.

The longest direct train link in the world now connects Moscow to Pyongyang, binding the authoritarian axis closer together. Taiwan remains the flashpoint. And American allies are watching, waiting to see if Washington can lead with clarity.

This is the chessboard. And the moves are happening fast.

YOUR ROLE IN THE WAR ALREADY UNDERWAY

If you are a CEO, a board member, a regulator, or a manager, **you are on the firing line**.

Your decisions—where you invest, where you source, which markets you prioritize—affect not just your company's future, but the outcome of this contest. **You have contributed to China's rise, often unknowingly.** Now you can help break its march.

As these industries are destroyed, middle managers disappear. They must become aware and put their efforts into rebuilding American manufacturing.

But I know what you are thinking. I hear it in every boardroom I enter: *"We can never catch up with China."* Some CEOs say it bluntly: *"It is inevitable."* You see China's scale. Its subsidies. Its coordination. You conclude the fight is over.

Let me tell you: **That is exactly what President Xi wants you to believe.**

Because if you believe China is inevitable, you will not act. You will not extricate. You will not diversify. You will not rebuild. And China wins by default.

But here is the truth: **China's model has weaknesses.** It is built on currency manipulation, subsidies that cannot be sustained indefinitely, and an authoritarian system that suffocates individual initiative and stifles the very innovation it seeks to replicate.

America and its allies have strengths China cannot match—capital discipline, technological creativity, trusted institutions, and the rule of law. And yes—**reverse choke points.** China cannot build advanced semiconductors without Taiwan's TSMC, the Netherlands' ASML, and US-based Applied Materials. China's rare earth processing depends on specialty chemicals and precision equipment controlled by the American Sphere. China's chemical refineries need catalysts that it cannot replicate.

The question is not whether America can win. The question is whether America will coordinate.

WHY I WROTE THIS BOOK

I wrote this book with two purposes.

First, to expose the underpinnings of China's strategy using facts most people are not aware of. Once you understand how the 90 Percent Model works, how currency manipulation sustains it, and how encirclement strategy is executed, it is impossible to dismiss the threat. It is also impossible to ignore the brilliance of Xi's execution.

Second, to skip the hand-wringing and jumpstart actions governments and corporations can take to change the course.

This is not a book of lamentations. It is a playbook.

Part I shows you what China is doing. Part II shows you America's strengths and why the tide is turning. Part III gives you the "Counterattack: Urgent, Determined, Coordinated"—the detailed, industry-specific, step-by-step actions that governments and businesses must take to break China's model within three to five years.

These are not abstract recommendations. They are **practical actions** I have refined over 60 years advising the world's largest companies. My clients have executed them. They work.

Will my recommendations be accepted? I do not know. But I do know this: **What has been tried so far has failed. And doing nothing is not an option.**

A FINAL WARNING

October 10, 2025, will be remembered as the day China declared economic war on the free world. Most people didn't notice. Most leaders still haven't.

But the war has already begun.

The boards of every major corporation must discuss the upcoming risks. Not someday. **Now.**

Ask yourself:

- **Has your Chinese competitor built hyperscale excess capacity, taken over 50 percent market share, and driven your unit costs up?** This is the most solid signal you need to change track and protect yourself. The data is available. Use it.
- **Do you have a war room tracking early warning signals?** Or are you flying blind until the earnings call?
- **How is your competitor poaching your employees, particularly technology people?** Are the offers targeted? Systematic? Coordinated?
- **Do you have CCP members on your board or in key positions?** If yes, your strategy is visible to Beijing.
- **Are they pushing you toward a joint venture or asset sale?** Understand: What you give up, you will never recover.

And if you think this is just General Motors's problem, or Boeing's problem, or Intel's problem—think again. **You could be under the bus sooner or later.**

The intensity of this contest is accelerating. The months ahead will bring moves and countermoves that will reshape industries. And the companies that do not prepare will not survive.

THINK FOR YOURSELF

I know this sounds alarmist. I know some of you will dismiss it as hyperbole. But ask yourself: Did you know that China could shut down entire industries with export restrictions at will?

Did you know that the October 10, 2025, announcement was a watershed moment, a declaration of economic warfare?

Did you know that the US-China War is not temporary, not cyclical, but structural and existential? **And that there is no end in sight?** This is the contest that will define not just this decade, but this century.

The wake-up call has sounded.

The only question now is: Who is awake enough to answer it?

Will you be a casualty, or will you be a leader?

The choice is yours.

Ram Charan, December 2025

PART I

China's Strategy of Encirclement

Chapter 1

The 90 Percent Excess Production Capacity Model: The Heart of China's Playbook

America has an acute problem. It has a **chronic trade deficit** with China. Worse, China uses its trade surplus to demolish America's economic base and undermine the US-led world order.

When I say "China," I mean the Chinese Communist Party (CCP). That distinction matters. The CCP holds absolute control over capital, companies, people, and policy.

America is China's largest debtor. In 2024 alone, the US ran a **$300 billion trade deficit with China**, and nearly **$600 billion** if you include its shadow proxies: **Vietnam and Mexico.**[23] A significant volume of Chinese goods is routed through local factories in smaller countries (transshipments), many of them built, owned, or controlled by China, making the real exposure even deeper.

Since 2009, the US has run up a **$7.4 trillion** (see Exhibit 1: trade deficit) cumulative trade deficit with this network. With the annual gap still growing at roughly **5 percent** a year, this burden could reach **$12 trillion** by 2030 and exceed **$16 trillion** by 2035.[24]

I urge you to reflect on what this means. This is not America's federal deficit, money we owe ourselves. This is wealth transferred to a rival systematically destroying America's industrial base. **It is deadly.**

A large part of this deficit is concentrated in just four sectors: **machinery, electronics, vehicles, and pharmaceuticals**. The spine of any modern economy (see Exhibit 1: sectoral imbalance[25]). But look beyond them, and the picture grows starker.

Apparel, furniture, toys, beverages, iron and steel, aluminum, and plastics also run deep deficits. There is no natural reason for these products to be imported at such scale. They are not the result of genuine competitive advantage but of **China's deliberate 52 percent currency devaluation**—from 4.8 renminbi (RMB) per dollar in 1990 to 7.3 in 2024 (see Exhibit 2: currency disparity[26])—and the use of **artificially depressed prices** to undercut competitors.

Recalibrate the system, and there is no reason why America and its allies cannot rebuild these industries. They carry no choke points, yet they are staples of daily life, and their erosion leaves Western populations dependent when they should be self-reliant.

The US runs persistent trade deficits with allies too—the EU, Japan, South Korea, Canada, and Taiwan—that further widen its industrial gap. In fact, these five partners alone account for over **$500 billion**, or **42 percent**, of America's $1.2 trillion total trade deficit in 2024 (see Exhibit 1: regional imbalance[27]). Yet the China-linked deficit remains the largest, fastest-growing, and most dangerous.

The **paradox** is that most of these countries are **friendly democracies**, yet their deficits compound the problem. China, the fierce opponent, amplifies the damage by leveraging indirect routes and gaps in the system. The point is clear: America must bring these **offenders**, friendly or otherwise, into line.

Exhibit 1: The Dire Reality: US Trade Imbalance with China, Its Proxies, Even Allies

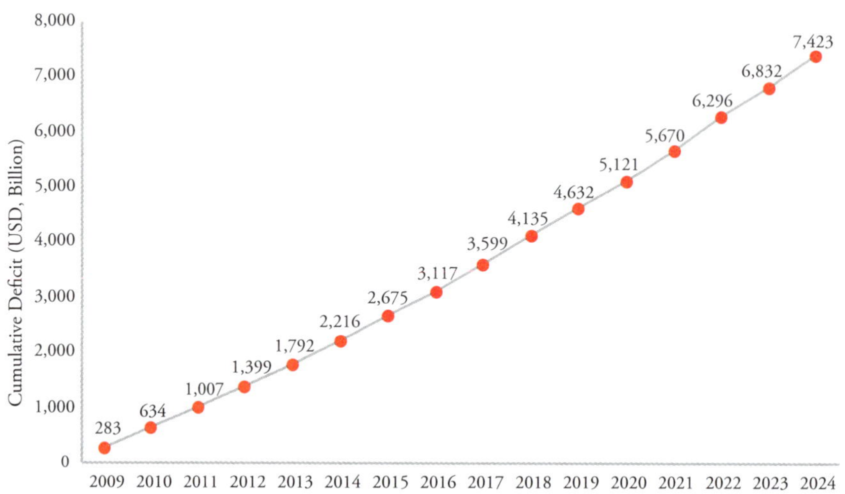

Source: United States, Census, Bureau

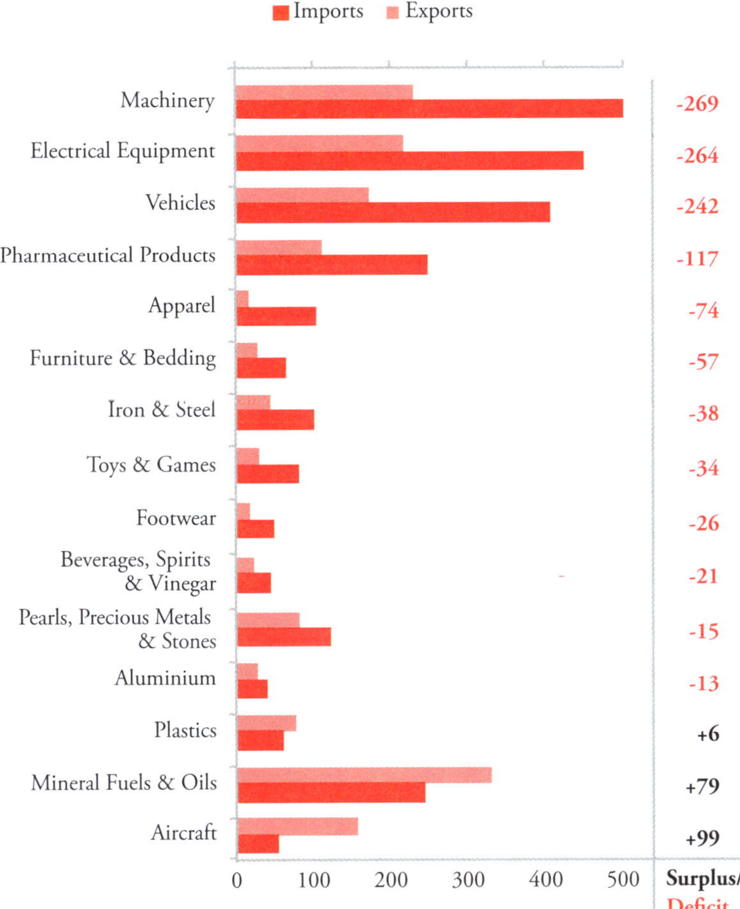

Source: *The Wall Street Journal*
Note: Regional breakdowns exclude trade partners that had less than $5 billion in combined US imports and exports in 2024. Regional groupings are based on World Bank classifications, with some groups combined for display purposes. Goods category names are simplified from the two-digit level of the Harmonized Tariff Schedule; aircraft and vehicles includes parts; electrical equipment includes electrical machinery, electronics and parts; furniture and bedding includes light fixtures; toys and games include sports equipment.

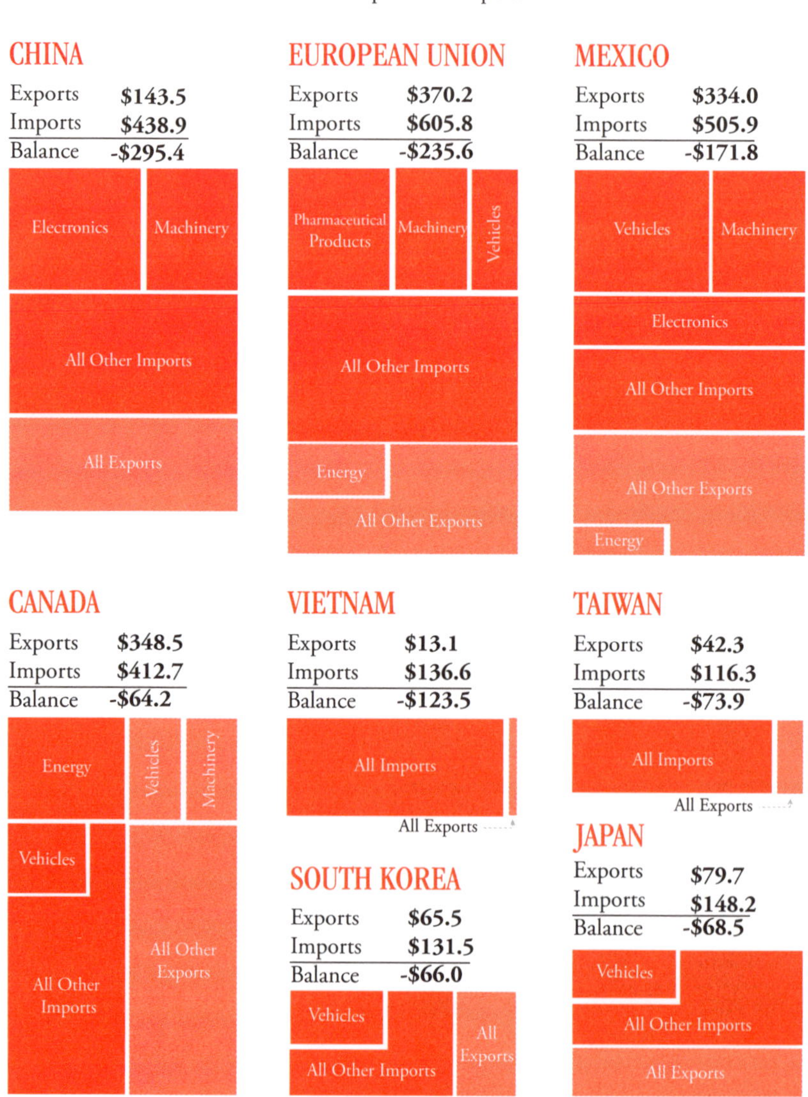

Source: *The Wall Street Journal*
Note: Machinery includes nuclear reactors, boilers, mechanical appliances, and parts. Vehicles include vehicle parts. Electronics include electrical machinery and equipment, sound recorders and reproducers, television image and sound recorders and reproducers, and parts and accessories. Energy includes oil, gas, and electrical energy.

CHAPTER 1

THE 90 PERCENT MODEL: CONTROL, NOT PROFIT

At the heart of this problem is what I call the **90 Percent Excess Production Capacity Model**. It is not a theory or interpretation. It is a deliberate pattern of state-driven industrial dominance that has played out in industry after industry. President Xi carried the torch passed down from Deng Xiaoping to Jiang Zemin to Hu Jintao and scaled it beyond anything his predecessors envisioned.

Why 90 percent? In my work across China—with Chinese, American, and European executives alike—I have repeatedly heard this number as the aspiration. Not a statistical threshold, but a mindset: Dominate global capacity so thoroughly that no competitor survives without China's permission.

The idea is simple but deadly. Here's how it works:

> **Identify a key industry, build hyperscale capacity to produce 90 percent of global demand, and flood the market at marginal (the cost of producing one additional unit) or below variable cost pricing. Then push prices even lower by exploiting a chronically undervalued currency (see Exhibit 2: currency disparity), giving Chinese exports an artificial edge. All of this is funded by almost unlimited subsidies drawn from China's trillion-dollar trade surplus. No one can compete against this model.**

The result? Entire industries collapse. Companies disappear. And whole towns or even states are economically ravaged.

Return on capital is irrelevant. As one Chinese executive told me bluntly: *"If we don't have the money, we don't pay. If we need help, the Party steps in. Suppliers will merge or cut prices—we make it happen."*

Beijing lets a brutal contest play out inside China itself: dozens of firms competing, losing money, scraping for survival. Once one emerges with scale or technological edge, the state crowns it a **champion**—pours in contracts, credit, and protection—and then sends it into global markets, armed to destroy the next industry in its path.

Global dominance and control, not profit, is the objective.

And that's why the CCP will not give it up easily. The 90 Percent Model is a core pillar of Xi's geopolitical power. Breaking it would mean dismantling the foundation of China's global ascent. He will **fight to protect it at all costs**.

Exhibit 2: China's Currency Games

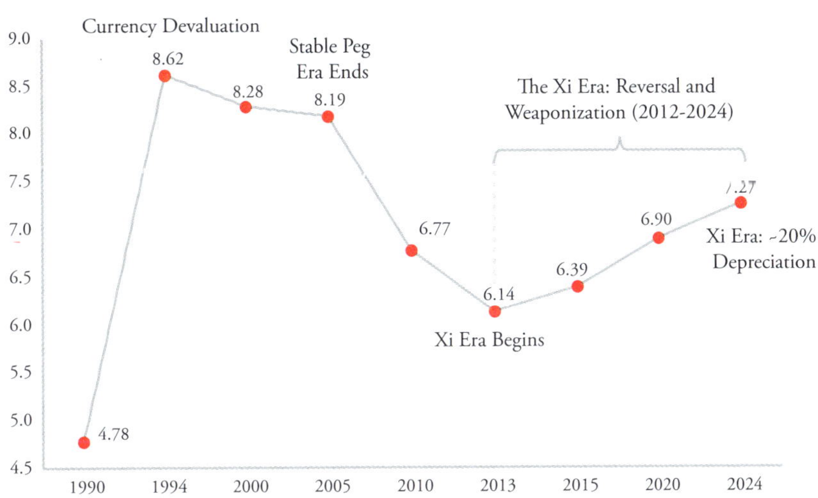

Phase	Key Insights	Purpose
Currency Devaluation (1994)	Sharp devaluation. An ~80% drop in RMB against the dollar.	Establish China as a low-cost manufacturing powerhouse.
Stable Peg Era (1994–2005)	Exchange rate held steady at ~8.28 through tight government control.	Lock in export competitiveness. Resist international pressure to appreciate.
Managed Appreciation (2005–2013)	Gradual, controlled RMB appreciation under international pressure.	Appear responsive to global concerns while carefully protecting export industries.
The Xi Era: Reversal and Weaponization (2012–2024)	Deliberate devaluation of ~20% that reversed prior appreciation gains.	Weaponize currency to sustain export dominance, fund the 90 Percent Model, and maintain trade surplus advantage.

Source: Author's analysis, IMF, World Bank, People's Bank of China

THE FALLOUT: 10 DOWN, 10 TO GO

This model has already **wiped out or marginalized at least 10 major industries** in the US, including furniture, textiles, toys, and consumer electronics.[28] Entire regions—Michigan, Ohio, Pennsylvania—have been devastated. The next wave is already underway: EVs, renewables, advanced agriculture, maritime equipment, biopharma, new materials, advanced rail transit, aerospace, artificial intelligence, and robotics. These are the 10 sectors named in the *Made in China 2025* plan.[29] And they are being **targeted with precision** (see Exhibit 3: industrial destruction).

Exhibit 3: 10 Industries Targeted. 10 Destroyed.

Made in China 2025—10 Targeted Industries

Industry	Focus Areas
Next-Generation Information Technology / Artificial Intelligence	AI, IoT, Cloud Computing, Semiconductors
Robotics & High-End Automation	Industrial Robots, Service Robots, Automation Systems
Maritime Equipment & High-Tech Ships	Ocean Engineering, High-Tech Ships
Advanced Rail Transit Equipment	High-End Speed Trains, Smart Transportation System
New Energy Vehicles & Equipment	Electrical Vehicles, Fuel Cells, Autonomous Driving Technology
Power Equipment	Smart Grid Technology, Renewable Energy Equipment

Advanced Agriculture Machinery	Smart Farming Equipment, Agricultural Technology
New Materials	Advanced Composites, Rare Earth Materials, High-Performance Materials
Biopharma & High-Performance Medical Devices	Advanced Medical Equipment, Innovative Drugs, Biotech
Aerospace and Aeronautical Equipment	Aircraft, Space Systems, Aviation Technology

Source: Centre for Strategic and International Studies

10 US Industries Destroyed by the 90 Percent Model

Industry	Examples
Furniture	Home, Office, Outdoor Furniture
Toys	Children's Toys, Dolls, Scooters
Consumer Electronics	Phones, Small Appliances, Game Consoles
Basic Chemicals	Bulk Chemicals, Industrial Inputs
Solar Panels / Photovoltaics	Modules, Wafers, Cells, Polysilicon
Rare Earth Processing	Magnet Processing, Rare Earth Refining
Textiles / Apparel	Garments, Fast Fashion, Fabric Processing
Pharmaceutical Ingredients	APIs, Generics, Core Ingredients
Lithium Battery Manufacturing	EV Batteries, Cell Manufacturing
Telecom Infrastructure	Mobile Networks, Switching Gear, Core Systems

Source: Author's analysis

The destruction of these industries follows a deliberate design. It reflects a **structural asymmetry**. The American system asks firms to deliver quarterly returns, protect shareholder value, and obey antitrust constraints. The Chinese system, by contrast, consolidates national purpose through industrial war, using companies as instruments—not ends. That is the true imbalance at the heart of this contest.

WEAPONIZING GLOBAL TRADE SURPLUS

The model is not isolated to the US. It is executed widely with Europe, Southeast Asia, Latin America, Africa—anywhere China can build and extract surplus.

The result is a relentless surge in China's global trade surplus—$1 trillion in 2024 alone (see Exhibit 4: trade surplus). Since 2009, **Beijing has amassed $7.5 trillion in hard cash** from trade partners. At its current pace of **11 percent** cumulative annual growth, the surplus could exceed $16 trillion by 2030 and $29 trillion by 2035.[30]

That surplus is being reinvested not only into the next cycle of excess capacity but also into military-civil fusion research and infrastructure deals across more than 100 countries. China turns cash into dominance—acquiring ports, minerals, markets, and votes.

Follow the money, and the timeline becomes clear. Xi took power in 2012, but the first three years were base-building: consolidating control, purging rivals, setting the stage. **The systematic**

assault began in 2015. That's when China's industrial policy sharpened, subsidies intensified, and the 90 Percent Model moved full throttle. **By 2018, the rocket launched.** Trade surpluses that had averaged $200–300 billion annually exploded to over $800 billion by 2022 and hit $1 trillion in 2024. That **seven-year surge, 2018 to 2025**, is when China's surplus accumulation reached full velocity. The cash you see in Exhibit 4? Most of it came from this concentrated seven-year period.

Looking through the lens of President Xi, it is a **brilliant** strategy executed with discipline, and clearly **succeeding.** China has every right to pursue its national interests. But the effect has been to put America and its allies in a deep quandary.

Exhibit 4: Hard Accumulated Cash from Global Trade Surplus

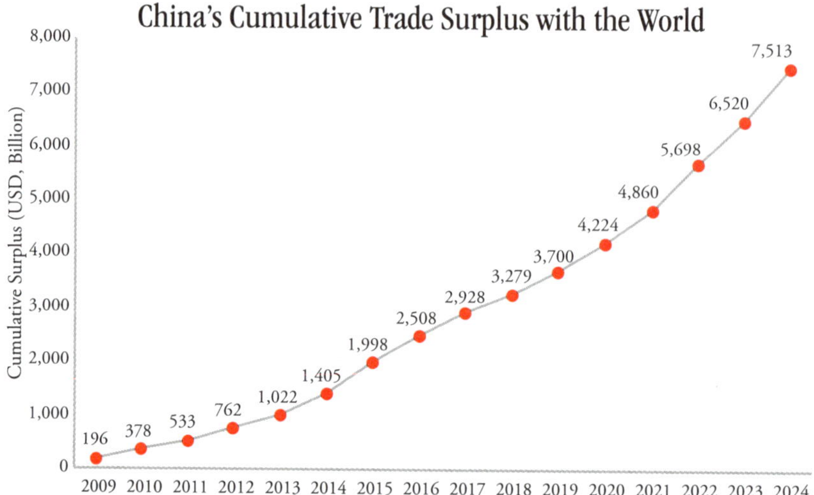

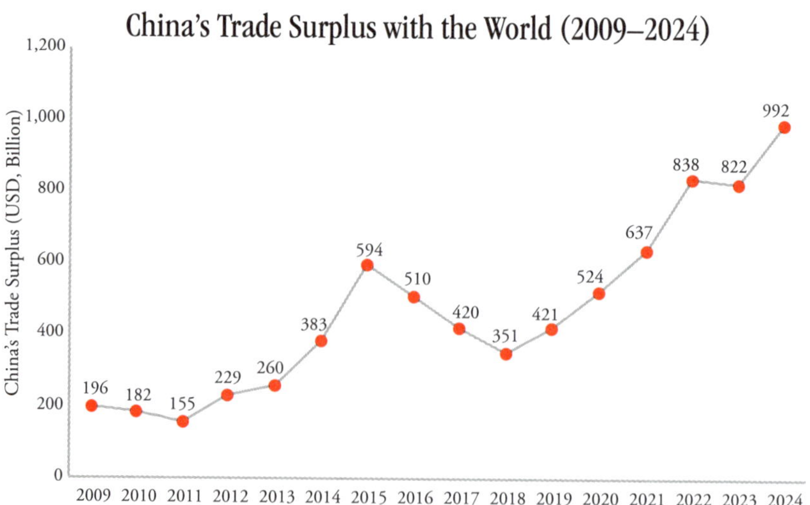

Source: World Bank, Statista

WHY THE OLD TRADE RULES NO LONGER WORK

This is not how the postwar economic system was supposed to work. The original architecture relied on **two assumptions**: that countries would trade based on comparative advantage, and that currencies would self-correct to rebalance trade.

But neither assumption ever fully worked. The heads of nations like Japan, Germany, South Korea, Canada, and Taiwan used privileged access to the American market to build their economies and amass surpluses.

In some cases, **US presidents even helped in the early stages**, especially with China, and later ignored the warning signs. This was never the internal trade once practiced among allies. Once China entered and manipulated the system, the flaws became glaring. Beijing exploited the loopholes left by the World Trade Organization (WTO), laissez-faire exchange policy, and fragmented Western governance.

INSIDE THE WEB: A SYSTEM OF ENTRAPMENT

Inside the US, the effect of the 90 Percent Model is everywhere (see Exhibit 5: 90 percent entrapment[31]). China is deeply **embedded in every walk of American life like a spiderweb**. They are inside the arteries of American commerce—digitally, financially, and physically. The numbers tell the story:[32]

- **China produces almost a third of global manufactured goods**—more than the US, Germany, Japan, and South Korea combined.
- Yet it consumes just **15 percent** of what it produces. That's not a flaw. It's the model.
- In **730 of 5,000 globally traded product categories**, China accounts for more than **50 percent of world exports**—three times more than the EU, and nearly **eight times more than the US**.

China continually **invents new methods using AI to advance manufacturing**; it now commands the steepest AI-driven experience curve on the factory floor.

You see it in daily life: **90 percent of US microwaves** come from China. So do **three-quarters of phones, game consoles, and small appliances**. China makes **75 percent of American toy imports**—dolls, scooters, tricycles. Even Mattel still produces **40 percent of its global output** there, despite tariffs remaining punishingly high.[33]

And it's not just end products. China now dominates **critical inputs**, the raw materials, components, and manufacturing capabilities that underpin modern life and national security. These aren't just economic assets. They are potential **choke points**. A single export ban could freeze Western industries, paralyze supply chains, and weaken military readiness. The warning lights are already flashing.

Consider just a few examples:

- **Rare earths:** China refines 85–90 percent of global rare earth elements and produces 92 percent of rare earth magnets essential for missiles, aircraft, EVs, and electronics.[34]
- **Lithium-ion batteries:** China controls 60–90 percent of the entire supply chain across mining, processing, cell components, and battery assembly.[35]
- **Solar panels:** China holds over 80 percent of global production, even while many suppliers operate at crushing debt and cash losses.[36]
- **Pharmaceuticals:** China controls roughly 80 percent of the global supply of generic active pharmaceutical ingredients.[37]
- **Defense metals:** Nearly 80 percent of US weapon systems rely on materials like antimony, gallium, and tungsten—all dominated by China.[38]
- **Chemicals:** China controls nearly 40 percent of global chemical sales and is a top exporter of base chemicals, polymers, and critical inputs like dyes, solvents, and specialty intermediates vital to both industry and defense.[39]

This is not overreliance. **It's entrapment.** And it's already underway. China has used its choke hold on rare earths to win relief on US tariffs, deferred thrice as of August 2025. It is a glimpse of how quickly these levers can be pulled and the damage they can inflict.

If these choke points are not a national security issue, then what is? In wartime, a pandemic, or any major shock, every factory lost and every capability surrendered erodes not just industry but the nation's ability to survive. This is an existential threat.

Exhibit 5: The 90 Percent Entrapment

Global Trade Dominance:

US vs. China

In 2000, US, trade totaled $2.0 trillion—more than four times China's $474 billion. From 2000 to 2024, US trade expanded by 167% (4.2% CAGR), while China's trade surged by 1,200% (11.3% CAGR), surpassing the US in 2012. By 2024, total trade reached $5.3 trillion for the US and $6.2 trillion for China.

■ US as the Larger Trading Partner ■ China as the Larger Trading Partner

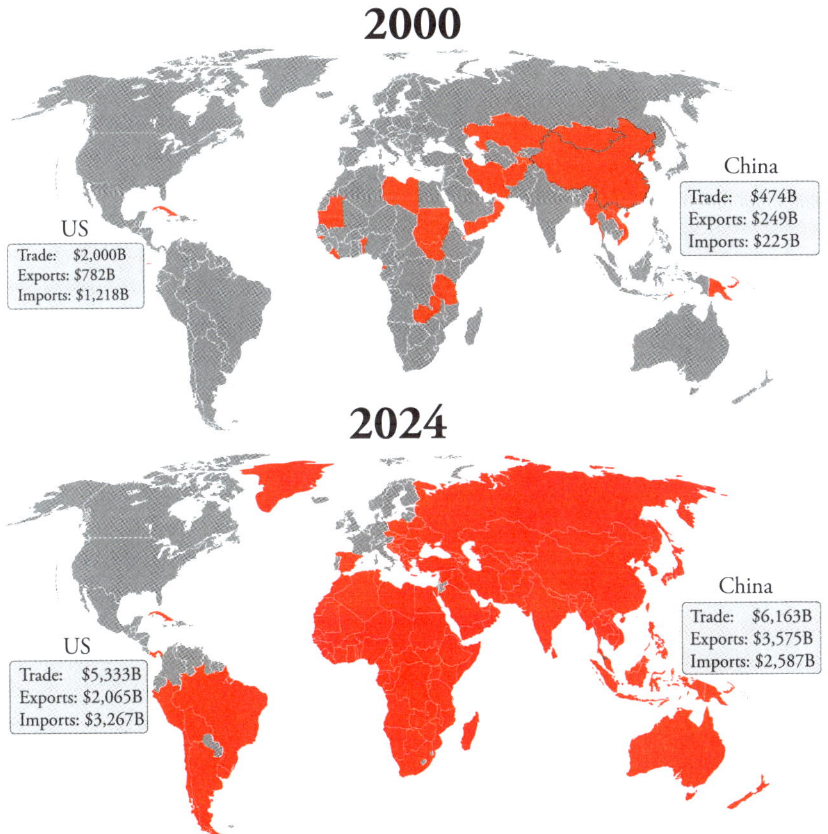

Merchandise trade = exports plus imports
The data on US trade partners is sourced from the US Census Bureau, and data on China's trade partners comes from the General Administration of Customs.

Source: Visual Capitalist: "How China Overtook the US in Global Trade (2000–2024)"

MY VIEW AS A STUDENT OF STRATEGY

Before we dive into the next chapter, I want to pause and give you my take. You have just seen the facts. But here is how I see it, as someone who has spent decades inside boardrooms, watching strategies unfold in real time. This is a global economic war that has been **silently raging** for nearly two decades. And now, for the first time, the very heart of President Xi's strategy is under direct attack.

1. **Xi's engine is finally in full view.** For the first time, the 90 Percent Model sits under a spotlight bright enough for every CEO, policymaker, and ally to see. Until now, no US president—not Clinton, Bush, Obama, or Biden—has put that engine on the table. Trump has. Henry Kissinger, the former US secretary of state who engineered the opening to China in the 1970s and remained Washington's most influential strategist on Beijing for five decades, believed America's central task was to decide what it truly wanted from China. For the first time, that choice is being quantified, with a methodology to confront it, even if many dislike the approach.
2. **This is a clash of two leaders, not two countries.** I have watched many brutal fights for market share; they always come down to the will and resolve of the two people at the top. **Leaders compete; nations follow.** Today it is Xi versus Trump, each wielding near-absolute authority over totally different governance systems. That level of personal power is

expected in an autocracy like China. What's extraordinary is that it's now matched, for the first time, by a US president operating within a democracy.

3. **Xi's core bet just broke.** He assumed a divided America would never produce a president willing, or able, to hit the CCP at the center of its power. Tariffs, tech bans, and a $1 trillion trade-surplus squeeze have shattered that assumption.
4. **Xi now faces a worthy opponent, and he knows it.** The US has begun targeting the 90 Percent Model directly. Xi has tools—exploiting choke points, weaponizing prices, and leveraging currency disparity—but for the first time, those tools are being watched, measured, and challenged.
5. **The next phase is coalition pressure.** To finish the job, Washington must lock arms with Europe, Japan, India, and the $60 trillion American Sphere (specifics in Chapter 10). A July 2025 deal with Vietnam imposed a 40 percent tariff on transshipped Chinese goods aimed at blocking backdoor routes.[40] Expect similar clauses in future trade pacts. If allies join in and stop absorbing China's overcapacity, the 90 Percent Model hits a wall.
6. **Currency disparity is the invisible engine.** Unless addressed, the trade deficit will never shrink meaningfully. China's export advantage is baked into the yuan's long-term undervaluation (see Exhibit 2: currency disparity). Tariffs

are the most immediate tool to offset that imbalance. But tariffs alone are not the endgame. This period must be used to rebuild domestic capacity in the US and among its allies. Without that self-sufficiency, the leverage from tariffs will fade, and the deficit will return.

7. **Expect relentless tit-for-tat.** This is hand-to-hand economic combat. Tariffs here, export bans there. This is the new normal. There will be emotion, missteps, and backtracking. President Xi, like Mao before him, seeks what Mao called a *"strategic stalemate"*: an enduring, manageable equilibrium in which American pressure becomes tolerable and time works in China's favor. It will be a long game. A **race to the bottom**, where each side tests limits without triggering collapse. And there is **no silver bullet**. Only resolve, coordination, and sustained pressure over time.

This is where we stand: two systems, two leaders, and one global economic war now fought in daylight. The 90 Percent Model is no longer hidden. The onslaught is active, deliberate, and escalating.

Behind it all is a **single operating mind.**

In any war of this scale, leaders go to extreme lengths to assess the opponent. In the next chapter, we look beyond the model to the **man who powers it,** President Xi Jinping—his character, his motivations, his doctrine. Because if you want to dismantle a system, you must first understand how and why it was built.

Chapter 2

Xi's Modus Operandi: Decoding His Operating Code

When two rivals grapple for supremacy, the one who wins is usually the one who predicts best—the opponent's behavior, intent, actions, and threshold of pain. Prediction, in turn, rests on observed behavior. Facts, not slogans, reveal his intent.

The 90 Percent Model is alive and accelerating. It remains the beating heart of China's playbook, driving surplus, strangling competition, and powering its global rise. But to truly understand what we are up against, we must look past the model itself and study the man who is directing it.

THE MOMENT THE MASK SLIPPED

In February 2012, during his visit to the US, then–Vice President Xi Jinping traveled to Washington, Iowa, and Los Angeles. He met with President Obama and Vice President Biden, and in his public remarks, Xi emphasized China's ambition to build globally recognized brands, names that would appear on shelves around the world, just as American brands had for decades. This wasn't a passing comment. It reflected the core of Xi's life project: **Dethrone American industrial preeminence and install Chinese names in its place.**

That purpose didn't emerge from personal ambition alone. It sits on a foundation laid decades earlier. The blueprint goes back to Deng Xiaoping's 1978 visit to Singapore,[41] where he saw how a small nation had vaulted from third world to first through state-led capitalism. Lee Kuan Yew, Singapore's founding premier, had combined political control with global trade, logistics mastery, and hard-currency accumulation. Deng internalized the formula and scaled it to continental proportions. Chinese mayors were soon being sent to Singapore for boot camps under Lee's mentorship. From Singapore to Shenzhen, the DNA is visible.

But Deng's genius was not just in copying Singapore. He picked up the Lenin torch that had fallen with the Soviet collapse. He benchmarked Lee Kuan Yew's economic model. He trained mayors methodically. He laid low. And most importantly, he built a **new economic strength model**, one superior to his opponent's, and quietly restarted the march of communism. The insight was clear: Economic strength, once higher than America's, would result in political accomplishment and the spread of Lenin's ideology. That the economic strength is being used to challenge America is now abundantly clear.

Deng's model was later hardened by his successor, and Xi's predecessor, Hu Jintao. Rush Doshi—director for China on President Biden's National Security Council—documents in *The Long Game* how, in the 1990s, Hu launched a grand strategy to blunt American power and shift the global order in China's favor.[42]

Drawing on original Mandarin-language Party documents, Doshi shows how the pivot came after what he calls a *"traumatic trifecta"*: Tiananmen Square, the Gulf War, and the Soviet collapse. Hu feared that Western liberalism, consumer excess, and free expression could corrode Party discipline and threaten the CCP's survival. His solution was three-fold: build self-sufficiency, enforce absolute Party control, and raise a modern military capable of withstanding a US strike.

Xi inherited that scaffold in 2012 and decided he would finish the job. Openly, rapidly, and under his personal command.

In 2015, he unveiled *Made in China 2025*—a manifesto that listed the industries to be conquered one by one: semiconductors, EVs, aerospace, biotech, advanced rail, AI, and more. The plan married Hu's self-sufficiency doctrine to an explicit production mandate to out-scale foreign rivals.

XI'S SIX CONVICTIONS THAT DRIVE EVERY DECISION

Xi's actions look sprawling only until you recognize the underlying beliefs. He has six convictions that lock together like cogs:

1. **The US ultimately wants regime change in China.** Any concession that weakens Party control is an existential risk.
2. **Information is a virus.** Western media, apps, universities, and even joint ventures carry liberal contagion. Firewall everything.
3. **One captain, one compass.** Pluralism shattered the Soviet Union. Inside China, there will be no competing factions. Only hierarchy, reinforced by surveillance and preemptive purges.
4. **Trade surpluses are ammunition.** Hard-currency reserves finance technology catch-up, foreign influence, and, if necessary, wartime imports.
5. **Allies are clay, not stone.** Europe can be tempted, Southeast Asia divided, and democracies distracted. Fracture coalitions before they cohere.
6. **Democracies cannot win.** No stability of leadership. Constant political churn. Deteriorating institutions. The time to overpower is now.

Once you see that grid, every headline—whether a port acquisition in Africa or a rare earth embargo threat—snaps into place as an execution detail.

FROM FEAR TO AUTOCRACY: THE PERSONAL POWER PLAY

Xi devoured case studies on the Soviet collapse and drew a ruthless lesson: Competition inside the ruling class breeds coups; openness breeds unrest; scarcity disciplines the masses. He abolished term limits, packed the Politburo with loyalists, and launched the most sweeping purge since Mao. Between 2012 and 2022, nearly five million officials had been investigated, jailed, or disappeared.

Surveillance became the other pillar. Today China fields roughly one camera for every two citizens, plus phone metadata, facial recognition, and social-credit scoring. The message is unspoken but universal: *Think twice; we are watching.*

Xi paired repression with **austerity**. He resurrected a Mao-era slogan—*"Thrift is glorious"*—and ordered cadres to lead by example: fewer banquets, plainer suits, no champagne. The point was behavioral, not economic. A population conditioned to scarcity will not rebel when sanctions bite.

President Xi runs China like a **single conglomerate**, driven by a strict system of fear, punishment, and consequence. He behaves not like a statesman balancing institutions, but like an **autocratic CEO**:

consolidating control, enforcing discipline, and punishing those who don't deliver.

This is not a democracy with checks and balances. This is a **command structure** (see Exhibit 6: Xi's Command Structure[43]). Xi sits at the apex as general secretary, chairman of the Central Military Commission, and state president. Below him, the Politburo Standing Committee—**seven loyalists**—controls every lever of state power. From the 205-member Central Committee down to 2,296 National Party Congress delegates, authority flows in one direction: downward. Every strategic decision—from rare earth exports to semiconductor subsidies to port acquisitions—requires his approval. This is corporate hierarchy taken to its logical extreme: **absolute authority, zero dissent, total execution**.

Exhibit 6: Xi's Command Structure—The CPC Hierarchy

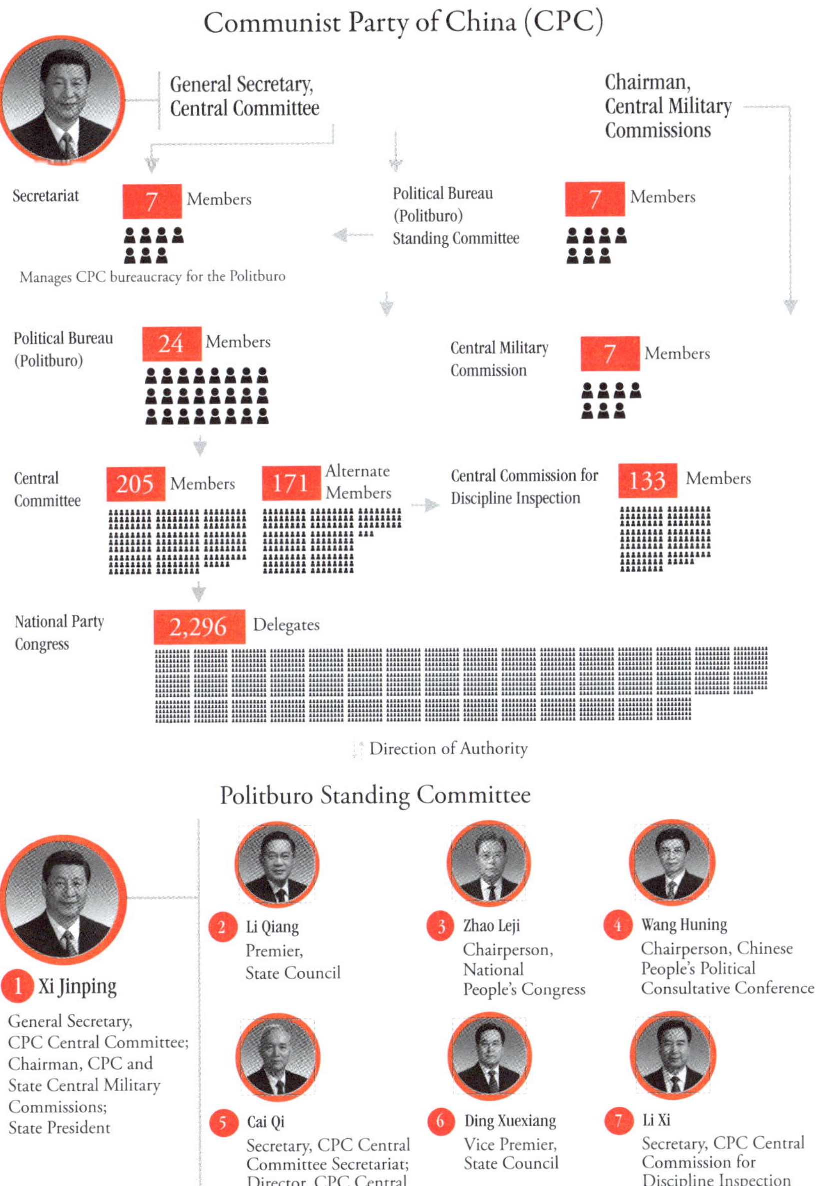

Source: CRS graphic by Mari Y. Lee, based on data from the Communist Party of China's news portal, http://cpc.people.com.cn/. Note: CPC Politburo Standing Committee members are listed in rank order; current as of January 1, 2025.

With this structure in place, Xi executed methodically (see Exhibit 7: Xi's strategic decisions). Each decision built on the last, consolidating authority while expanding China's reach.

Exhibit 7: Xi's Execution Timeline (2012–2025): From Consolidation to Global Dominance

Year	Decision/Event	Impact
2012	Ascends to power as CCP General Secretary	Launches anti-corruption campaign, cements personal authority
2013	President of China, major economic reform agenda	"Comprehensively Deepening Reform"—market and social reforms
2014	National Security Commission and new cyber controls	Comprehensive surveillance, increased security focus, internet governance
2015	Launch of *Made in China 2025*	Strategic manufacturing upgrade for self-reliance
2017	"Xi Jinping Thought" in Party Constitution	Institutionalizes ideological dominance and long-term political vision
2018	Removal of presidential term limits	Enables Xi to remain in power indefinitely
2020	Assertive COVID-19 management, global health role	Expands state control, demonstrates crisis management, leverages health diplomacy
2021	Declares "Moderately Prosperous Society," Dual Circulation Strategy	Focuses on domestic resilience and global supply-chain influence
2022	Emphasis on self-reliance, third term as leader	Further centralization, tech and supply-chain security
2023+	Expands global initiatives (BRICS, SCO, GDI, GCI)	Asserts China's role in shaping global governance

Source: Author's analysis

The pattern is unmistakable: **First, consolidate internal control (2012–2014).** Purge rivals, establish surveillance, cement authority. **Second, launch the industrial offensive (2015–2018).** *Made in China 2025*, ideological dominance, removal of term limits. **Third, expand globally (2020–2025).** COVID-19 crisis management, dual circulation, BRICS and Shanghai Cooperation Organization (SCO) expansion. This is not improvisation. This is the execution of a master plan.

BUILDING THE ARSENAL: COMPANIES, LOGISTICS, AND FORCE

Global champions. That 2012 promise of Chinese brands became a state mandate. Local firms were ordered to scale until they could command nine-tenths of global demand. Losses were irrelevant; market share was the only key performance indicator (KPI). Once a domestic *"winner"* emerged—Huawei in networks, CATL in batteries, BYD in EVs—the Treasury, state banks, and provincial subsidies flooded in. Export prices dropped below Western cost curves. Competitors bled; Wall Street applauded *"efficiency"*; and Xi harvested the surpluses and foreign direct investment (FDI).

Logistics choke points. Factories alone do not guarantee dominance; arteries do. So, Beijing underwrote ports in Gwadar, Piraeus, and Lamu; rail lines across Eurasia; fiber-optic cables in the Atlantic; and a constellation of logistic data hubs managed by

Chinese software. Every corridor shortens China's supply lines and lengthens America's.

A revved-up military engine. Money from trade surpluses pours into *dual-use labs*—hypersonics in Wuhan, quantum comms in Hefei, carrier-killer missiles in Guangdong. Xi's goal isn't to match the Pentagon tank for tank. It is to make US intervention so costly, dangerous, and politically unpopular that America hesitates to act at all. He has said **he does not want to fire the first shot**. A Chinese academic captured Xi's doctrine perfectly: *"China will not fire the first shot, but China will not allow you to fire the second shot."*[44] Pressure on Taiwan, the Philippines, and others is designed to distract, divide, and pull them closer to Beijing—much as in World War II, when misdirection kept opponents guessing where the blow would land.

Behind each investment lurks a personal habit: Xi chairs more than a dozen **Leading Small Groups (LSGs)**. Bodies that cut across ministries, bypass formal state bureaucracy, and bring data and options directly to him. These groups consolidate power at the top and enable Xi to make decisions that shape decades, not just quarters. He signs off on semiconductor subsidies, port leases, and even TikTok algorithms. Nothing strategic moves without his nod.

CHAPTER 2

DIVIDE, DISTRACT, EXHAUST: THE PERIPHERAL PLAYS

This is Mao's playbook: Win from the periphery to the center. But Xi is doing both at the same time. While the industrial machine hums, Xi keeps opponents off-balance.

He whispers sweeteners to Europe—tariff waivers here, rare earth *"green channels"* there—while punishing Lithuania or Australia the moment they break ranks. He buys discounted Russian oil, financing the Ukraine war, knowing it drains US attention and ammunition budgets. He courts Saudi Arabia with yuan-denominated oil settlements that nibble at dollar primacy.

He is using BRICS (Brazil, Russia, India, China, South Africa), alongside other blocs and bilateral alliances, to build pressure points against the West and present alternatives to US-led institutions. In July 2025, taking a dig at Trump, Brazil's President Lula put it bluntly: *"The world has changed. We don't want an emperor."*[45]

Xi's success with India reveals the **psychological dimension** of this strategy. Despite deadly border clashes in 2020 and ongoing territorial disputes, India continues participating in BRICS summits and SCO meetings. Prime Minister Modi attended the SCO summit in Tianjin in September 2025, his first visit to China in seven years, while maintaining bilateral trade discussions with Beijing. Xi has convinced New Delhi that engaging China is pragmatic statecraft, that India can balance between Washington and Beijing, **hedging rather than choosing.**

Every flare-up forces Washington to split bandwidth: new sanctions packages, fresh carrier deployments, emergency appropriations. **Distraction is a strategy, not a by-product.** China will not attack Taiwan unless the Chinese mainland is struck first. Xi has said he **doesn't want to fire the opening shot**. Instead, like the Allied deception that misled Hitler about where the D-Day landing would occur, he applies pressure on Taiwan, the Philippines, and others to pull them closer into Beijing's orbit, forcing the US and its allies to prepare for blows that may never land, and stretching resources all the same.

MY TAKE: XI'S OPERATING CODE

Xi's counsel to the Party apparatus is one of patience. He has demonstrated the power to shape global outcomes. He choreographs every negotiation with Trump—timing, stagecraft, nothing left to chance. Delays, sanctions, and even tactical retreats are tolerable side effects, so long as they wear down the opponent over time. Beijing's intent is clear: Play hardball, drag it out, and exhaust the other side.

One cannot underestimate the determination and strength of President Xi as a strategist. His ability to execute has been amply demonstrated, and the impact of his initiatives is already visible not just in America but across its allies. He is playing for the long haul.

CHAPTER 2

In any prolonged contest, the lead shifts back and forth. Battles are won and lost, but endurance decides the outcome. The side that can best anticipate its opponent, force adjustments, and test resolve is the side that prevails. Sometimes exhaustion sets in, sometimes determination breaks. As in chess or a long tennis match, the pressure mounts with time, and the chance of **stalemate** rises. Global rivalry is no different. America and China may clash, maneuver, and trade blows for years, yet still land in an equilibrium—an uneasy coexistence born not of victory, but of endurance.

This is the strategic interdependence John Nash described: Neither side can win outright, so both must continuously assess the other's threshold for pain and adjust accordingly.

This is why **Xi will defend his machine to the last yuan**. Beneath its vast scale lies fragility. If the surplus shrinks, subsidies falter. If subsidies dry up, overcapacity collapses. And if the 90 Percent Model dies, the illusion of inevitability that holds the Party together begins to crack. Xi knows it, and that is why he will fight at every turn, tolerating sanctions, setbacks, and tactical retreats to keep the **long game alive**.

Xi's ultimate mission is to impose CCP ideology on the world, **whatever it takes**, short of direct and intensive military conflict with the US. It is the organizing principle behind every decision: surpassing the West in military and industrial strength, encircling it through controlled logistics and data flows, fracturing its alliances, and funding it all through the 90 Percent Model's trillion-dollar surplus. Based on

Lenin's principle, executed with autocratic precision, and driven by fear. **It is brilliant. It is cogent.** And it is aimed directly at ending American primacy.

WHERE WE GO NEXT

The next four chapters break open the machine, each revealing a core pillar of Xi Jinping's offensive architecture. If you understand these, you understand the levers that must be pulled to reset the balance:

- **Creating Globally Dominant Chinese Companies**
  How China has used foreign know-how to build its own world-scale firms that undercut prices and dominate global markets.
- **Controlling Global Flow: Trade, Logistics, and Data**
  The arteries of China's global reach—from ports and undersea cables to digital infrastructure and trade choke points.
- **Weaponizing Technology: The Rise of China's Military Machine**
  How commercial tech, state subsidies, and IP theft are being weaponized to create a modern fighting force.
- **Waging War Without Firing a Shot**
  How Beijing wages a soft war by distraction (lighting many fires all over the world) and distortion (waging psychological warfare).

Chapter 3

Creating Globally Dominant Chinese Companies

Ten industries targeted. Ten industries marginalized or destroyed. This is how China did it.

The reality, as we saw, is that China is run like a multinational corporation, and **President Xi is its CEO for life**. He has no shareholders to answer to. No regulators to constrain him. No opposition of any kind to slow him down. His authority is **absolute**, and his mandate is clear: to upend the American-led global order by building dominant industrial strengths that surpass, and eventually displace, those of the West.

This is also an act of survival to maintain the viability of the CCP in a way the Soviet Union could not. Xi studied the Soviet collapse closely: Economic stagnation, the inability to compete globally, and the failure to generate hard currency killed the USSR. China's industrial strategy is designed to avoid that fate.

This is not capitalism as we know it. It reflects the logic of communist philosophy: top-down, autocratic, and personally directed. Every decision, from factory permissions to foreign acquisitions, rolls up to the center. And every actor in the system knows the goal: **Build hyperscale that is modern and efficient, integrate vertically, and dominate globally.**

President Xi selects the industries he wants to control—telecom, EVs, solar, infrastructure—and moves with speed. State capital floods in. Local governments compete to host. Permits and subsidies flow. The mission is to **capture global market share at industry level, even at a loss**—through volume, marginal-cost pricing (abated by undervalued currency), and speed.

And this isn't limited to the giants. Thousands of small and midsized firms follow the same playbook—state-backed, globally ambitious, and operating below the radar. Together, they extend China's industrial footprint deep into the global economy.

These firms are built to dominate. And they cannot be understood through Western business logic. **Put yourself in the opponent's shoes**, or you will misread the game entirely. Western executives assess China using their own playbook: return on investment, capital efficiency, shareholder value. But in China under President Xi, these metrics don't exist. Only one goal matters: **global market share dominance.** Cash losses are tolerated. Subsidies are strategy.

Negative returns for years? Acceptable, if it means capturing the world.

Xi has nurtured **Darwinian competition** within China's borders, letting firms fight brutally for survival in targeted industries, then backing the winners with unlimited state support. These champions aren't drilled for efficiency but for supremacy.

In China, your opponent isn't the firm across the table. It's the CCP itself. The Party sets the rules, regulates the terms, and changes them at will. Your China strategy works until it doesn't. Until the day you have transferred your technology, your talent, your operational know-how, and the CCP decides it's time to push you out. **You don't control the shelf life of your China strategy. The CCP does.**

THE SCOREBOARD

This is what Chinese state-backed dominance looks like in practice:

- **DJI** controls over 90 percent of the global consumer drone market.[46]
- **CATL** is the world's largest EV battery maker, powering everything from Tesla to European commercial fleets.[47]
- **Haier** has displaced legacy American and European brands in appliances across key markets.
- **CRRC** manufactures 44 percent of the world's trains, dwarfing all competitors.[48]

- **WuXi AppTec and WuXi Biologics** now dominate the outsourced pharma manufacturing space. They serve all of the top 20 global pharmaceutical companies and support over 1,000 active clinical trials.[49]
- **Chinese chemical producers** now account for more than 40 percent of global basic chemicals output, tightening control on precursors essential across critical industries.[50]

These are not just successful exporters. They are state-aligned champions scaled with speed, backed by subsidies, priced with currency disparity, and built to capture global market share while rewiring supply chains in China's favor.

FILTERING STARTS AT HOME

Before any of these firms go global, they are put through a **brutal process of internal filtering**. President Xi's 2015 plan launched simultaneous waves of investment across key sectors—EVs, solar, semiconductors, advanced manufacturing. Dozens of firms were funded in parallel, but with no safety net.

The logic was simple: Let market forces and engineering realities do the weeding. No bailouts, no protection. Only one goal. Find the player with a dominant scale or a clear technical edge. Then back that winner with full state support and let the rest collapse.

Solar is a prime example. One of my Chinese clients in the sector went bankrupt twice in 30 years. The CCP used internal competition as an engine of industrial Darwinism. What survived was leaner, faster, and battle-hardened. Ready for global assault.

CHINESE INDUSTRIES ON THE ATTACK

Some industries aren't just economically important; they are **weapons of attack**. China has turned industries such as pharmaceuticals, chemicals, and telecom infrastructure into instruments of strategic assault. These sectors power hospitals, militaries, supply chains, and everyday life. When a foreign power dominates them, **it controls your sovereignty**.

This is **a deliberate national security threat**, designed to create dependence that becomes leverage in a crisis.

China understands what many Western leaders have missed: Control over these industries is control over nations. And they have spent two decades building that control systematically, sector by sector, choke point by choke point.

Let us start with pharma.

Today, China produces a majority of the world's active pharmaceutical ingredients (APIs), the essential components that power antibiotics, antivirals, and basic medicines. Reports suggest that the US is dependent on China for 33 percent of API capacity and 80 percent of key starting materials (KSMs) for biotech inputs and drug development.[51]

It's not just the low-cost antibiotics or generic drugs. China also leads in the production of key precursor chemicals for cancer therapies, anesthesia, and cardiovascular treatments. As one senior US official put it, *"If China shut the door tomorrow, our hospitals would be empty in weeks."*

At this point of writing, this capability sits entirely in President Xi's hands. He can restrict exports from any of these industries at any moment, and he has already demonstrated this power by imposing restrictions on rare earth magnets, forcing immediate policy concessions. Xi has effectively placed **monitoring controls on critical Western industries.** He can activate restrictions at will, and the West has no immediate alternative supply.

In the chemicals industry, the story is just as stark.

Chemicals are the foundation of almost all industrial production across every country, directly impacting consumers in everything from soap to smartphones. They underpin pharmaceuticals, plastics, textiles, agriculture, electronics, and defense systems. Without a functioning chemical sector, modern economies grind to a halt.

And China dominates it. China controls upstream and midstream chemical production—everything from basic feedstocks to specialty inputs used in semiconductors, EVs, defense coatings, and industrial catalysts. In 2024, China accounted for 56.5 percent of global fine and specialty chemical sales, more than the US, EU, and Japan combined.[52]

The result: Western firms have downsized or exited entirely. Olin shut major US chlorine and chemical plants, citing high costs and overseas competition. BASF shuttered ammonia units and sold off high-value pigment divisions. In Europe, LyondellBasell and Tronox have closed Rotterdam plants, blaming Chinese overcapacity.

This is about controlling the scaffolding of modern industry, the materials that enable production in every sector. And what makes this more dangerous is the concentration. In both pharma and chemicals, production is increasingly consolidated among a handful of large Chinese players with deep state backing, opaque corporate structures, and zero obligation to remain neutral in a crisis. (See Exhibit 8: raw material dominance.[53])

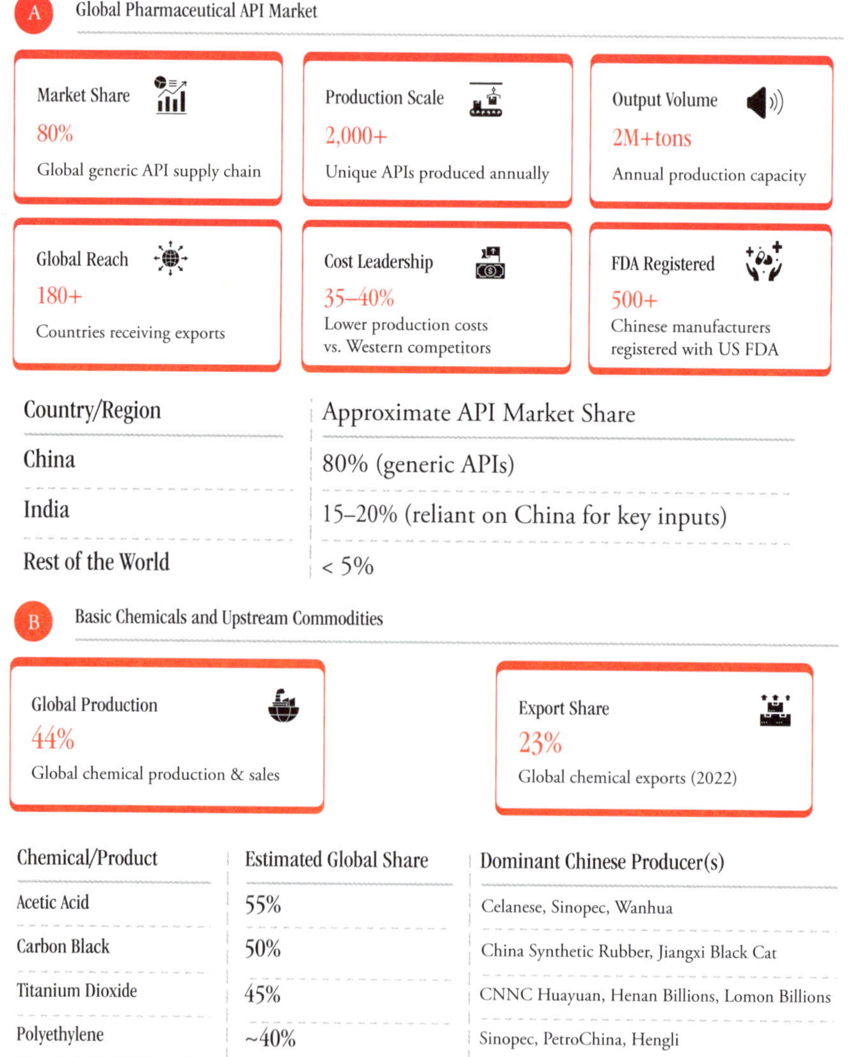

Country/Region	Approximate API Market Share
China	80% (generic APIs)
India	15–20% (reliant on China for key inputs)
Rest of the World	< 5%

Chemical/Product	Estimated Global Share	Dominant Chinese Producer(s)
Acetic Acid	55%	Celanese, Sinopec, Wanhua
Carbon Black	50%	China Synthetic Rubber, Jiangxi Black Cat
Titanium Dioxide	45%	CNNC Huayuan, Henan Billions, Lomon Billions
Polyethylene	~40%	Sinopec, PetroChina, Hengli
Generic APIs	80%	Numerous firms (e.g.,WuXi AppTec)

Strategic Implications

Supply-Chain Vulnerability:
Virtually all global manufacturers rely on Chinese inputs for critical pharmaceutical and chemical building blocks

Systemic Risk:
Interruptions, export controls, or policy changes in China could disrupt entire global supply chains

Unprecedented Concentration:
No other country matches this degree of upstream control in any critical sector

Strategic Advantage:
Decades of systematic capacity building have created seemingly insurmountable competitive moats

Sources: Industry analysis reports, FDA registration data, chemical industry trade publications, government policy documents, international trade statistics, and company annual reports

And it doesn't stop here.

The same playbook applies to telecom infrastructure. Devalued currency. Cheap equipment. Rapid deployment. Deep market penetration. Once installed, it becomes the nervous system of a country's communications,-and a potential vector for surveillance, disruption, or control.

A deeper look at China's targeted destruction of telecom infrastructure is a sample of its strategy and tactics. Consider the case of Huawei.

HUAWEI: A CHAMPION BUILT BY DESIGN

The telecom sector didn't fall behind by accident. It was targeted systematically by a nation-state with an aggressive plan.

Go back 25 years, and the scoreboard looked very different. Motorola, Lucent, Cisco, and Nortel were the major players shaping global telecom infrastructure. These were the firms that helped build the internet. By 2010, most were bankrupt, acquired, or irrelevant. What happened wasn't market drift. It was industrial displacement, orchestrated from Beijing, executed through Huawei.

Huawei wasn't built in a garage. It was constructed, step-by-step, by a state that knew exactly what it wanted. When the US banned telecom exports after Tiananmen, China responded not with retreat, but with resolve. It would build its own national champion. The CCP offered Huawei land, capital, contracts, and political cover. But the real advantage was subtler: a direct pipeline to Western know-how.

Eager to access China's growing telecom market, firms like Motorola, Lucent, Nortel, and Cisco were pushed into joint ventures. They opened R&D labs in China. They trained local engineers. They hosted subcontractors on-site for months at a time. Managers taught manufacturing, quality control, and even marketing. **It wasn't passive IP leakage. It was institutional knowledge transfer**—coordinated, organized, and complete.

Huawei recruiters literally pitched tents outside Lucent's New Jersey campus, offering 200 percent salary bumps. Meanwhile, Chinese engineers rotated through foreign R&D labs, absorbing decades of IP, process, and design capability.

Not all of it was voluntarily shared. In 2007, a Motorola engineer was caught boarding a one-way flight to China with over 1,000 internal documents.[54] Lucent had source code stolen. Cisco filed lawsuits. The US government eventually indicted Huawei on conspiracy, theft, and fraud. But the damage was done.

Lucent faded. Motorola exited. Nortel filed for bankruptcy. And Huawei, with full CCP backing, stepped into the global vacuum.

Today Huawei controls over 30 percent of the global telecom equipment market.[55] It is the world's largest equipment vendor by both revenue and share. Its equipment underpins networks across Africa, Asia, Latin America, and parts of Europe. Look at Exhibit 9: Huawei choke hold.[56] The red is sobering! And despite US pressure, much of the world still runs on Huawei hardware. Because it's cheap. And because the alternatives don't scale.

Exhibit 9: Global Dominance of Huawei Telecom Infrastructure

HUAWEI'S GLOBAL EXPANSION

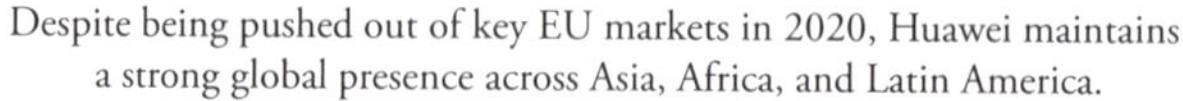

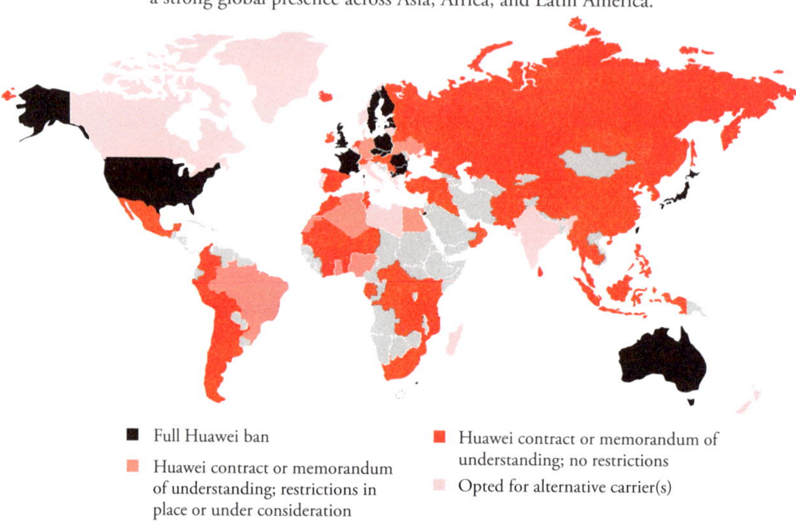

Sources: *Foreign Policy*, "5G Explained"
Note: Restrictions include banning Huawei from core network functions, placing Huawei under government security reviews, placing limits on the amount of Huawei equipment that can be used, limiting contract duration, or general government guidelines that urge telecoms to opt for alternative 5G carriers.

Let me remind the reader that telecom infrastructure is not neutral. As a senior industry executive bluntly said: "*It is a country's central nervous system enabling military coordination, emergency response, political dissent, and digital surveillance.*" Whoever controls it has the power to listen, disrupt, and influence. This is **entrapment**.

That's why, when one of Huawei's peers, ZTE, faced collapse under US sanctions, China's top leadership intervened directly. President Xi personally appealed to President Trump to lift US sanctions.

Because this wasn't about saving a firm. It was about protecting the backbone of China's expanding global footprint.

Huawei and ZTE now sit inside the networks of dozens of countries. Biden pushed allies to phase them out. Germany only recently announced a delayed removal, by 2029.[57] Meanwhile, the US itself no longer produces its own core telecom infrastructure. It relies on Ericsson and Nokia. China, by contrast, builds, controls, and exports its.

Word of caution: using cheaper equipment may look like a budgetary win. In reality, it can determine a nation's political destiny. Huawei and ZTE create **political-military-industrial control**: the ability to monitor, disrupt, and steer entire systems from within.

The Huawei playbook extends beyond telecom infrastructure. **Look at what happened with Nokia Networks.** It co-founded a joint venture with Huawei called TD Tech. Nokia brought the intellectual property, global reach, and industry standing. Huawei brought scale and state backing.

Over time, TD Tech became a Huawei proxy in all but name: Its leadership was ex-Huawei, and its products were based on Huawei designs. When Nokia tried to sell its majority stake, Huawei blocked the deal, threatening to revoke technology licenses and effectively vetoing the buyer.

Nokia was forced to exit on Beijing's terms. Huawei, together with state-owned entities, bought it instead. TD Tech now generates over $1 billion a year, runs in 100 countries,[58] and is effectively an extension of Huawei, funded by state entities and fueled by China's industrial playbook.

This is a blueprint replicated not just in China, but worldwide.

Huawei's rise was aggressive and state-led. Apple's story is more subtle, but no less revealing. Here, the transfer of knowledge wasn't extracted under pressure. It was handed over in pursuit of efficiency.

APPLE: PRECISION MANUFACTURING, TRANSFERRED IN PLAIN SIGHT

Apple wanted access to the Chinese market. To serve it, the company didn't just outsource assembly; it built the capability for it. In the process, Apple created an ecosystem of suppliers and taught them how to execute precision parts manufacturing at scale. Tolerances, tooling, line choreography, material science—it was all transferred. And **once that know-how spread, it couldn't be taken back.**

As Patrick McGee writes in *Apple in China,* when Apple first arrived, local manufacturers could not produce what Jony Ive's team had designed.[59] So, Apple brought the knowledge in.

Top engineers from Stanford, MIT, Dell, and Motorola flew to China to train local suppliers. They brought in manuals and machinery. They created playbooks. They taught on the line, side by side with workers. Some even slept on the factory floors.

This was **active capability building**, disguised as routine manufacturing. Beneath the surface flowed some of the rarest **tacit knowl-**

edge in modern industry: materials science, precision metrology, and clean-room discipline. Even the choreography of line changeovers.

Soon, factories like Foxconn became elite execution engines. Apple's tooling, quality control, materials science, and process innovations became embedded. What started as Apple's competitive advantage became **China's industrial base**.

And then something else happened. Apple imposed its **50 percent supplier constraint**. No supplier could depend on Apple for more than half of its revenue. That rule had profound second-order effects:

- It **forced Chinese suppliers to grow beyond Apple**, pushing them to win business from Samsung, Xiaomi, Oppo, Lenovo, and Huawei.
- It **triggered the horizontal diffusion** of Apple-grade process control across the ecosystem. The tacit know-how spread. Not the IP, but the discipline.
- It **accelerated China's dual-use capability**, where the same automation systems used for iPhones began enabling aerospace components, drones, and guidance systems.

Apple taught Chinese factories to walk, then pushed them to run. The result is a supplier base that no longer just serves Apple. It competes with it. Globally.

Apple believed it was optimizing for efficiency. But in reality, it was building **a manufacturing university**, and China graduated with honors. Soon after, Beijing turned that success into leverage, imposing regulatory pressure and quiet constraints that reminded Apple whose turf it was on. The ecosystem Apple built became a tool to humble its ambitions.

And Apple wasn't the only one. Tesla too entered China believing it was in control. Invited in, given red-carpet access, and allowed to scale. But what looked like a win turned into something else entirely: a playbook transfer that helped China build BYD into the world's most formidable EV challenger.

BYD: GLOBAL EV DOMINANCE, POWERED BY TESLA

Tesla's Shanghai Gigafactory was supposed to jolt China's EV market into higher performance, a *"catfish"* to make the other fish swim faster.

What happened instead? Within a year, China learned **how to build software-defined, hyperscale EV factories and to create entirely new EV models in under one year**.

Because the software is already built and tested, only the hardware needs design and manufacturing. The traditional 36-month development cycle is dead. What Tesla pioneered, China industrialized at scale. New models launch in months, not years. A speed that Western automakers cannot match.

Tesla taught Chinese automakers how to:

- Use software to rapidly improve hardware performance

- Update vehicles continuously, like app updates, not model years
- Optimize the factory through data feedback loops

And then China improved on it.

Beijing has poured an estimated **$231 billion in EV subsidies since 2009**, turning those lessons into scale.[60] In 2023 alone, Chinese brands sold 7.9 million EVs at home, giving them the volume base to underprice rivals abroad.[61]

BYD, once a fast follower, now outproduces Tesla in volume. It builds its own batteries, semiconductors, software, and motors. It's vertically integrated, globally ambitious, and cheaper than anyone else. And while Tesla presents itself as a partner, BYD is positioning itself as **the next dominant global player**. And BYD is not alone. NIO, Xpeng, Geely, and SAIC are following the same pattern.

Tesla was not just allowed in. It was **invited in**, to teach. Once the playbook was mastered and lavishly subsidized, its utility faded, and the shark began to feed.

This isn't about Tesla anymore. **The auto industry itself is the next battleground**. The West has already seen what happened in telecom and solar. Automotive is next. And Europe is seeing it first. Chinese brands are gaining share, opening showrooms, and undercutting legacy players whose cost structures can't adapt fast enough. In the US, the impact hasn't peaked yet, but the same structural vulnerabilities exist: high costs, fragmented supply chains, and slow adaptation to software-led manufacturing.

What's at stake isn't just car companies. It's the **entire industrial ecosystem around them: parts suppliers, software stacks, battery players, chipmakers**. Once those collapse, the recovery path isn't quarters. It's decades.

In November 2025, Ford announced that it is considering discontinuing the electric version of the F-150, its most profitable product line.[62] If the decision is finalized, it would leave America without a mass-market EV pickup in active production. A stark symbol of how quickly the automotive frontier is collapsing. Another American industry risks ceding ground, unable to match China's subsidized overcapacity and vertically integrated supply chains.

****

These stories follow a pattern. One repeated across industry after industry. Foreign firms enter China to access its vast market. They form joint ventures, transfer technology, train local teams, and build infrastructure. But once their domestic partners gain the know-how and reach scale, the game flips. Foreign firms are sidelined, squeezed out, or rendered obsolete.

I have seen this firsthand across aerospace, chemicals, rail, and medical devices. In one case, I am aware of a decision when GE was asked to transfer aviation technology to China. The Chinese pitch was clear: "*We are going to dominate this industry globally. You can either be a minority partner in a global winner or become a has-been.*" That pressure worked. Technology was transferred. The Chinese still haven't fully scaled the skills needed to make it work end to end. As one American engine producer told me, "*They can read the blueprints, but they don't know how to execute.*" **But they will get there.**

And President Xi is accelerating that timeline right now. In August 2025, China launched the K visa—a program targeting young foreign STEM talent with no employer sponsorship required, offering flexible entry and residence.[63] The timing is strategic: Just weeks after the US imposed a $100,000 fee on H-1B visas,[64] China opened its doors. Xi has authorized recruitment packages that many Western tech professionals cannot refuse. Subsidies, housing support, tax benefits, and long-term residency. This is not a future threat. It is happening now.

THE RISE OF THE INDUSTRIAL MIDDLE CLASS

So far, we have looked at China's global champions—the Huaweis, BYDs, and CATLs—and how they were scaled deliberately, often with help from the West. But beneath them, a quieter force has been building. A rising class of midsized Chinese firms. Since 2021, I have met regularly with 36 founders and CEOs of midsized Chinese companies—textiles, home goods, lighting, electronics—three times a year for two days. Their stories are remarkably consistent.

Their margins are collapsing. Inventories are full. Domestic consumption is weak. And they are now going global. Not to serve local customers, but to **use foreign bases to export back to the West.**

Mexico's and Vietnam's exports to the US have surged. Look closer, and you will find many of these factories are Chinese-owned. It's the same game, different geography.

Shenzhen offers rewards up to 2 million RMB for overseas construction projects and subsidizes up to 50 percent of expansion costs (legal, financial, insurance) with a cap of 20 million RMB.[65] President Xi has declared it strategic. Belts and Roads (specifics in Chapter 4) has shifted from megaprojects to **"small and beautiful"** operations in technology, health, and infrastructure partnerships led by small and medium enterprises (SMEs).

This is China's **industrial middle class going global** with coordination, incentives, and speed.

And a parallel push is happening inside China itself. The **"Little Giants" program** (see Exhibit 10: Little Giants sector focus[66]), launched in 2018, is backing thousands of innovation-led SMEs across sectors like robotics, biotech, aerospace components, and advanced manufacturing. These aren't household names. But they are fast, focused, state-supported, and increasingly global.

- Semiconductor laser producer **BWT Beijing** now exports to more than 70 countries.[67]
- Medtech firm **Endovastec** is active in 40 countries across Europe, Latin America, and Southeast Asia.[68]

- **Unicomp Technology**, which makes industrial X-ray systems, has reached over 60 countries.[69]

Exhibit 10: "Little Giants" Focus on Key Industries of the Future

The majority of Little Giant companies match the *Made in China 2025* priority industries

Share of Little Giant companies aligned with the *Made in China 2025* 10 core industries, by batch

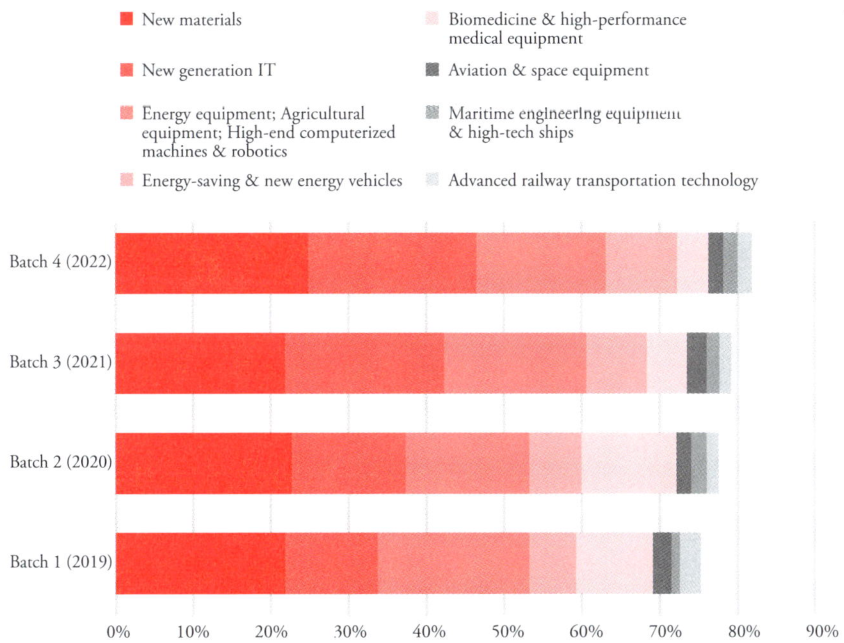

Sources: Sohu, Patsnap, Wind
Note: "Batch" refers to the selection round for Little Giant firms.

The exhibit reveals the strategic precision. The majority of Little Giants firms concentrate in the same 10 industries as *Made in China 2025*: new materials, next-generation IT, energy equipment, and robotics. These are **dual-use technologies** feeding defense, aerospace, AI, and semiconductors. Batch by batch, from 2019 to 2022, the program has certified thousands of firms, each one a building block in China's industrial war machine.

One midsized plant in Nairobi or a warehouse in Guadalajara might seem trivial. But replicate it 10,000 times, across 50 countries, and it becomes a powerful, distributed, and persistent presence. It is not flashy. It doesn't grab headlines. But it is real. And it is accelerating.

This outward push, whether through megafirms or agile SMEs, depends on something more elemental than just ambition and incentives. **Access to the raw materials that modern industry runs on.**

That's why China has spent two decades securing control over the most critical inputs, from rare earths to lithium to graphite, and the processing capacity that turns them into leverage.

Let us take a closer look at the critical mineral choke hold.

THE CRITICAL MINERAL CHOKE HOLD

Beijing has not only built factories, but also locked up the raw materials that those factories run on. Because in the modern industrial system, power doesn't just come from making the product. It comes from **controlling** the stuff that everything else depends on.

That's why **total vertical integration, from raw material extraction to final assembly**, is the foundation of China's industrial strategy.

And here too, the CCP plays a long game: a two-decade campaign to secure the world's most critical inputs, and the leverage that comes with them (see Exhibit 11: critical mineral choke hold[70]).

Exhibit 11: China's Choke Hold on Critical Minerals and Rare Earths

Examples of Rare Earth Element Uses

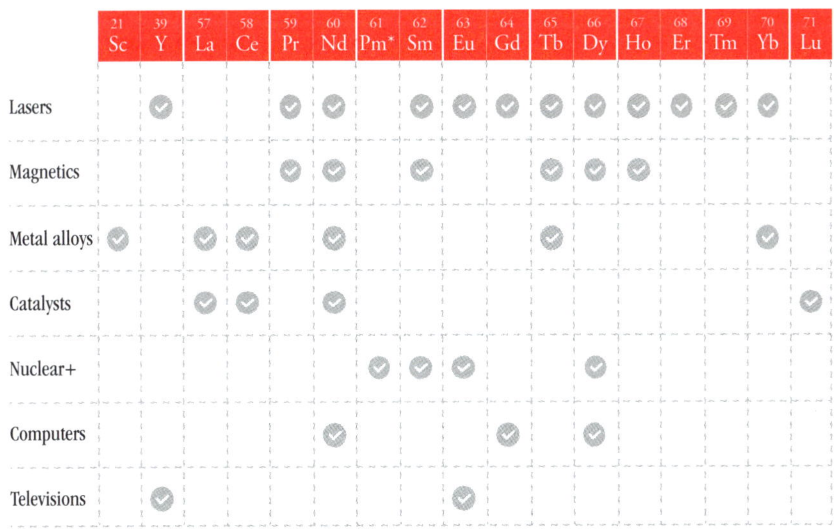

	21 Sc	39 Y	57 La	58 Ce	59 Pr	60 Nd	61 Pm*	62 Sm	63 Eu	64 Gd	65 Tb	66 Dy	67 Ho	68 Er	69 Tm	70 Yb	71 Lu
Lasers		✓			✓	✓		✓	✓	✓	✓	✓	✓	✓	✓	✓	
Magnetics					✓	✓		✓			✓	✓	✓				
Metal alloys	✓		✓	✓		✓					✓					✓	
Catalysts			✓	✓		✓											✓
Nuclear+							✓	✓	✓			✓					
Computers						✓				✓		✓					
Televisions		✓							✓								

*Not classed as a critical mineral by the US Department of Energy. +Reactors or batteries.
Note: Elements listed in order of Scandium, Yttrium, Lanthanum, Cerium, Praseodymium Neodymium, Promethium, Samarium, Europium, Gadolinium, Terbium, Dysprosium, Holmium, Erbium, Thulium, Ytterbium, and Lutetium.
Source : Virginia Department of Energy

Rare earth elements, estimated % of world total

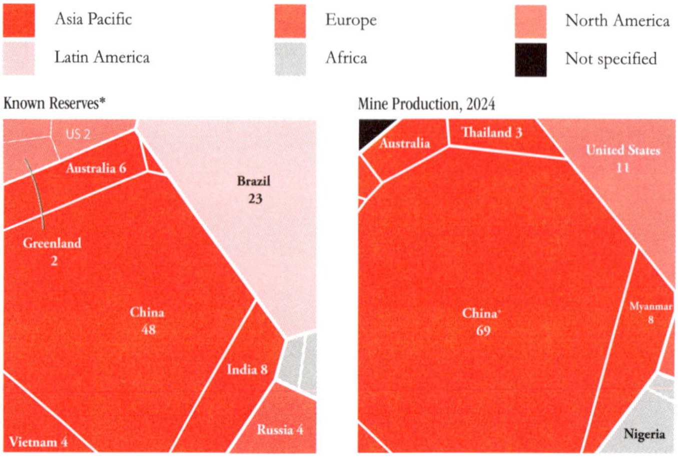

Asia Pacific
Europe
North America
Latin America
Africa
Not specified

Known Reserves*

US 2
Australia 6
Brazil 23
Greenland 2
China 48
India 8
Russia 4
Vietnam 4

Total: 90M tonnes of rare earth oxide equivalent

Mine Production, 2024

Australia
Thailand 3
United States 11
China+ 69
Myanmar 8
Nigeria

390K tonnes of rare earth oxide equivalent

*Countries and territories that have mapped out deposits in detail.
Data unavailable for Myanmar, Madagascar, Malaysia, and Nigeria.
+Estimate is a production quota and excludes undocumented production.
Source: USGS Mineral Commodity Summaries, January 2025

AMERICA'S IMPORT RELIANCE OF CRITICAL MINERALS

The US relies on a variety of nations to import critical minerals. How dependent is the US on imports for specific minerals, and which countries does the US depend on most?

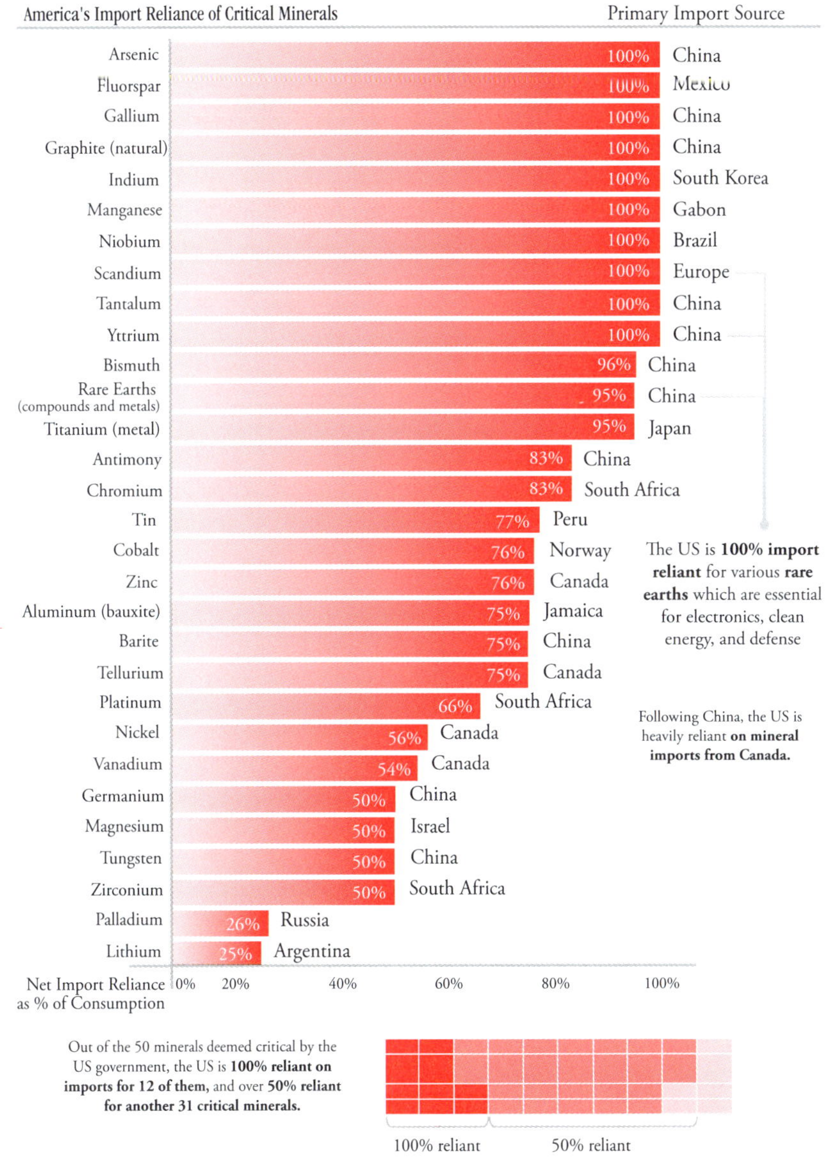

Sources: Visual Capitalist, "America's Import Reliance of Key Minerals"

This exhibit is President Xi's **comprehensive menu of choke points**. The first panel maps 17 rare earth elements across critical applications: lasers, magnetics, computers, nuclear systems, catalysts. Every checkmark is a potential export restriction. The second panel shows China's production dominance: **69 percent of rare earths, despite holding only 48 percent of reserves**. This proves control comes from processing capacity, not just mining. The third panel reveals America's vulnerability: **100 percent import reliant for 12 critical minerals** (including gallium, graphite, tantalum, rare earths), and over 50 percent reliant for 31 more. China is the primary supplier for most.

Xi has already **weaponized this choke hold** with rare earth magnet export restrictions. But magnets are just one element on the menu. Xi can activate restrictions on gallium (advanced chips), graphite (batteries), tantalum (electronics), yttrium (lasers), or any of the dozen minerals where America is 100 percent import dependent, whenever strategic interests demand. Without these inputs, missile systems, semiconductors, EV production, and fiber optics cease functioning. Modern defense and energy systems grind to a halt.

Demand is rocketing. The International Energy Agency projects that under current climate pledges, by 2040 demand will increase **fivefold for lithium, double for nickel and graphite, and grow 50–60 percent for cobalt and rare earth elements.**[71]

The greatest demand surge comes from **data centers**, the power-hungry infrastructure behind AI and cloud computing. Data centers and their supply chains consume rare earths at every level: neodymium for power generation, gallium and germanium for chips, yttrium for cooling, terbium for displays. The AI boom will drive demand far beyond these projections. Beijing prepared years in advance.

Made in China 2025 locked mineral security into industrial policy; state lenders funded refineries at home and equity stakes abroad. One example: In 2024, a CATL-led consortium signed a **$1 billion** deal with Bolivia to tap the Uyuni salt flats—part of the Lithium Triangle (Chile, Argentina, and Bolivia) holding 60 percent of global reserves.[72]

And while minerals exist across the globe, China controls what matters most—the ability to **process them**. That's where the true leverage lies.

Processing capacity is hard to replicate. It demands capital, infrastructure, environmental tolerance, and decades of technical know-how. China has spent the past 20 years building exactly that. Today, it **controls over 90 percent of global refining for rare earth magnets** and operates fully integrated supply chains—from upstream extraction to downstream conversion—while the US remains fragmented and overregulated.

The result is a choke hold. A form of economic coercion, built not through conflict, but through quiet, methodical control of the supply chain. The choke holds on critical minerals for the pharmaceutical and chemical industries are equally threatening to the well-being and national security of a nation.

Every critical material that China dominates, and the West depends on, is now a **live lever in trade negotiations**. That leverage will only grow as global demand surges.

Securing the world's critical minerals—every mine acquired, every refinery built, every global supply chain rewired—is backed by cash. The same cash that's funded the rise of megafirms, the global push of SMEs, and the subsidies behind scale. This is the **financial engine that powers China's global industrial dominance**. Let us look at how it was built and what it continues to drive.

THE CASH ENGINE THAT FUELS IT ALL

The 90 Percent Model is not just a weapon of price destruction. It is a **machine** engineered to generate enormous amounts of cash in hard currencies—dollars, euros, yen.

By flooding global markets with underpriced exports, China not only eliminates rivals but also **accumulates hard currency at industrial scale.** Dollars, euros, yen. The true currency of power. Unlike accounting profits, these reserves are liquid, portable, and potent. They fund the next wave of factories, subsidize strategic sectors, secure access to precious resources, and insulate against sanctions.

As seen in Chapter 1, in 2024 alone, China ran a **$1 trillion trade surplus** with the world, and it holds over **$3.3 trillion in foreign exchange reserves** (see Exhibit 12: Forex reserves), much of it in US Treasuries. Long-term US Treasuries form the largest component, the bedrock of China's reserve strategy. These holdings provide safety, liquidity, and ironically, leverage over the US itself.

Further, while China's officially reported US Treasury holdings have dropped sharply over the past decade, some analysts believe its true exposure is likely understated, as additional Treasuries may be held through custodial accounts in global financial hubs like Belgium and Luxembourg. Either way, China remains one of the world's largest creditors to the US government, giving it both leverage and potential vulnerability in financial relations.

On top of that, since 2008, over **$2 trillion in FDI** (see Exhibit 13: FDI flows) has flowed into China. Much of it from the very countries (e.g., US, UK, Europe, Japan, South Korea) now sounding the alarm. That capital helped scale China's factories, build its technology parks, and harden its industrial backbone.

Exhibit 12: China's Massive Forex Reserves

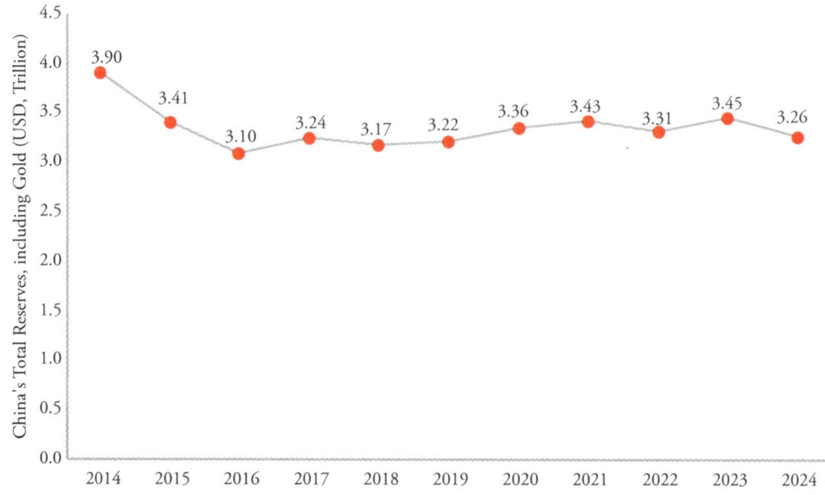

Source: World Bank

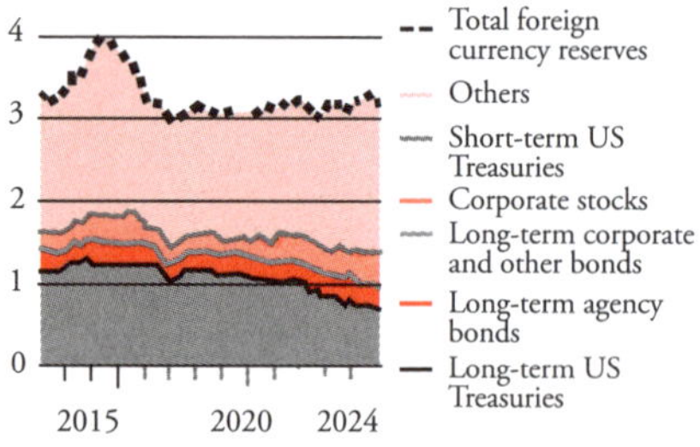

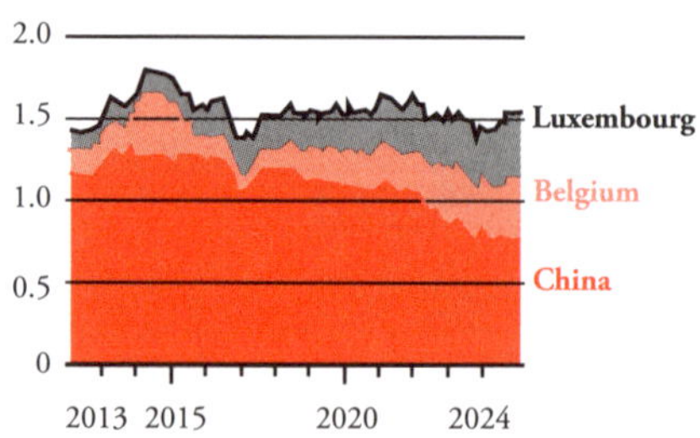

Data as of Dec. 2024. China may hold additional US Treasuries via custodial accounts in Belgium and Luxembourg.
Sources: China's State Administration of Foreign Exchange, Federal Reserve Board

Exhibit 13: China FDI Flows

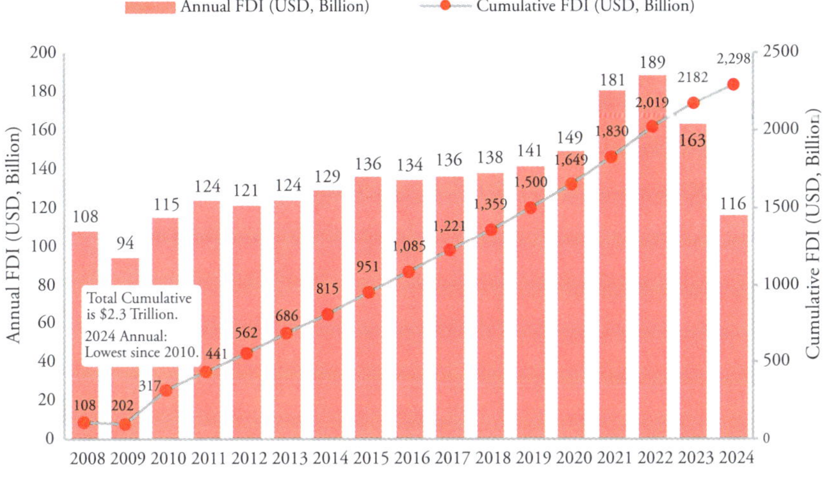

Source: China's Ministry of Commerce FDI Statistics–2024

Western capital helped fund China's growth. From the 1990s onward, multinationals offshored production to China to cut costs, preserve capital, and boost return on invested capital (ROIC). Many became dependent on China as a **single-source supplier.** Others tapped into cheap labor, cheap currency, subsidized land and construction, tax holidays, low-interest loans, and even energy subsidies to **improve margins**. Wall Street applauded. **Asset-light strategies** drove up stock prices. And in the process, billions in cash flowed into China's war chest.

Even after geopolitical tensions escalated, the flow didn't stop. In 2023, President Biden restricted US capital from reaching blacklisted Chinese firms. But that same year, **$6.3 billion** in US funds still made its way into them.[73]

The massive capital reserves that China has built are channeled into subsidies, R&D, state contracts, and acquisitions. **This is how the champions were built.** Funded by the West, trained by its multinationals, and then deployed to displace them.

MY TAKE FOR BUSINESS LEADERS

The march is on. China's state-backed firms are not just exporting; they are advancing with speed, scale, and improving quality. Over the last seven years, the **quality gap has closed dramatically**. AI deployment has accelerated this shift, with Chinese factories using artificial intelligence to drive productivity gains that compound quarterly. Their mission is not merely growth but to fulfill the CCP's goal: Achieve global dominance through companies that can dismantle the industrial base of the West.

These are not competitors in the traditional sense. They are instruments of state power, designed to alter the structure of global markets. If you are a board member, a CEO, or advising one, you must make **deliberate shifts in mindset and strategy** because the West has yet to catch up to the pace already set.

1. **The opponent is not a company, it's a system.** You are not competing with Huawei or BYD. You are competing with the CCP's ecosystem of subsidies, state-directed financing, labor controls, and export-driven industrial policy. Don't

benchmark against companies; benchmark against Chinese national policy.

2. **Marginal-cost pricing is not temporary; it's a way of life.** In key sectors—EVs, solar, semiconductors, telecom—Chinese players will continue to underprice global markets for years. If your strategy depends on pricing power, adjust your assumptions now.
3. **Protect tacit knowledge, not just IP.** It's not patents that matter most. It's process, routines, supplier relationships, and factory setup. Once transferred, this knowledge is permanent. Guard it.
4. **Future revenue streams are already under attack.** EVs, batteries, biotech, and green energy all sit squarely within China's target sectors. Watch the "Little Giants" program. These firms will take the market from below, quietly and fast.
5. **Secure your critical materials now.** Graphite, gallium, lithium, rare earths—if these are in your supply chain, start diversifying today. This is national security, not just procurement.
6. **Follow the money flows.** China's trade surplus and FDI inflows fund military modernization, talent recruitment, and state-backed acquisitions. Understand how your own capital may be contributing to your competitor's scale.

7. **Audit your incentives.** Many firms went into China to lift earnings, boost ROIC, and lower costs. That made sense, until it didn't. Are your current incentives blinding you to what's being lost?

This is not a normal market cycle. It's not a pricing war. It's **industrial encirclement**. If you are not planning for it, you are contributing to it.

A sobering note. *Prior to 2007, America and the West dominated global market share in 10 key industries that were marginalized or destroyed. Now China targets the next 10. The playbook is proven. Urgency is survival.*

Chapter 4

Controlling Global Flow: Trade, Logistics, and Data

China built globally dominant companies. Now it must ensure those firms have privileged access to the world's largest markets. Scale is useless without arteries. Once you build the firms, you must also control the routes—the ports, railways, cables, platforms, and data lines—that connect them to customers everywhere.

The goal is **zero dependence** on others for international access. China builds its own routes while remaining free to use everyone else's. But the access is one-way: China does not allow others equivalent use of Chinese-controlled infrastructure. This is **asymmetric control** by design.

I want you to picture a negotiating table. On one side sits an opponent who calmly repeats, *"What's mine is mine. What's yours is negotiable.*" President Kennedy once used that line to describe the Soviets, but it precisely captures the CCP's stance today.

Beijing fiercely guards its homeland markets, routes, and information with surgically sharp precision. Yet it cannot thrive without steady access to what other countries have: food, natural resources, energy, capital, and technology. China has found a way to play both sides. It controls its strategic dependencies on other nations by **owning the arteries through which everything flows**.

For over five decades, I have taught at Harvard Business School, advised many CEOs and boards, served on the board of a major Chinese company, worked with the founding leader of Baidu, and coached several Chinese CEOs. I have found that the best way to distill a company's strategy is to understand the actions already underway.

Now apply that principle to China. Follow the actions it is taking in logistics right now and put them in a broader context. Look at how they combine to form a key part of Xi's plan to upend America and its global order. These actions are detectable, and they matter for every global business.

A GEAR WITH THREE TEETH

Think of China's outward push as a three-toothed gear, turning in perfect synchrony:

1. **Trade routes**—to keep exports moving and dollars flowing in.

2. **Intelligence channels**—to harvest data and speed decision-making.
3. **Access levers**—to lock up raw materials and political alignment.

This gear gives China two decisive options: freedom to reach the world even in wartime, and power to slow or sever the flow for everyone else.

TRADE ROUTES: BUILDING THE HARDWARE OF ENCIRCLEMENT

Belt and Road, Version 2.0

Launched in 2013, the Belt and Road Initiative (BRI) began as a massive infrastructure rollout—ports, railways, roads, and power grids across the developing world. A decade later, the strategy has matured. What started as a construction campaign has evolved into a **control strategy of trade routes, logistics flows, and economic dependency**. This is Belt and Road, Version 2.0—less cement, more leverage (see Exhibit 14: BRI encirclement).

Exhibit 14: BRI, Global Encirclement

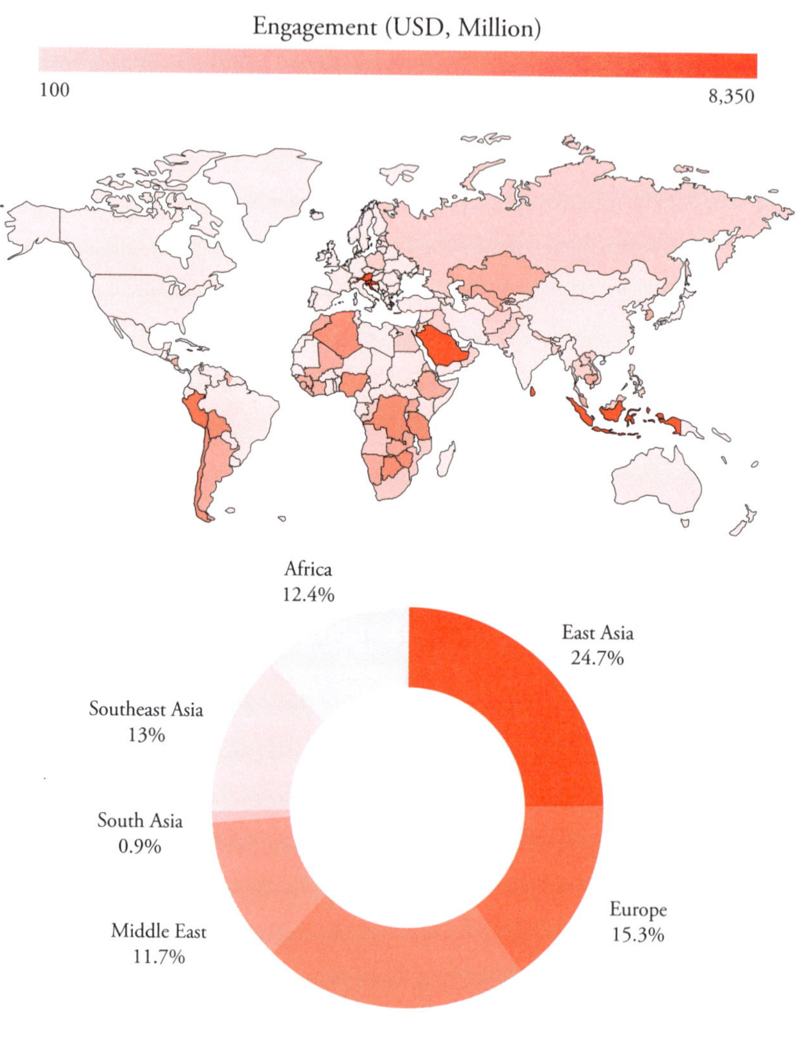

Source: Green Finance and Development Center, *China Belt and Road Initiative (BRI) Investment Report 2023*

The targeting is surgical. China concentrates investment where it cannot afford to lose access: Pakistan controls overland routes to the Indian Ocean. Indonesia commands the Melaka Gateway. The Middle East supplies energy. Latin America holds critical minerals. **Each dark zone on this map eliminates a strategic vulnerability**, a choke point that could otherwise be used against China.

Today, BRI touches nearly 150 countries and has driven an investment of more than $1 trillion into physical infrastructure.[74] A freight train can now leave northeast China and reach Europe in 16 days—half the time and cost it took a decade ago. Critics cite corruption, shoddy work, and unsustainable debt; Beijing quietly fixes what it must and moves on. The goal never changes: secure, faster, and China-managed pathways to global markets.

And this is not just about moving goods. It's about positioning. **Whoever controls access to the customer controls the terms of engagement.** Beijing is embedding itself deep into the commercial arteries of Africa, Southeast Asia, and Latin America—often by offering what the West won't: fast financing, fewer questions, and reliable delivery.

By selling into smaller economies and anchoring their logistics systems, China is building scale and tightening economic alignment. It gains both market access and lock-in.

Owning the Oceans

In 2024, Chinese shipyards delivered 53 percent of global commercial tonnage (see Exhibit 15: owning the oceans); US yards delivered one-tenth of 1 percent. A vessel that holds the equivalent of 3,600 20-foot containers costs $333 million to build in Philadelphia versus $55 million in Shanghai.[75]

Exhibit 15: Sea Power, Owning the Oceans

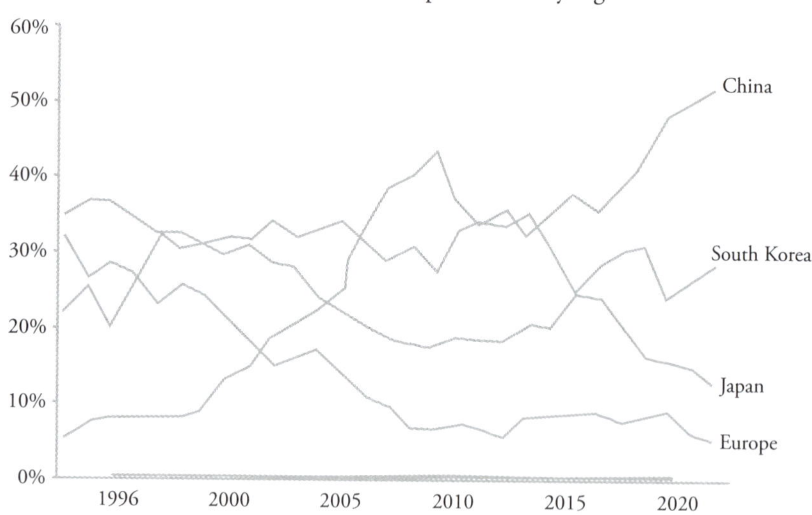

Source: Clarksons Research
Note: By compensated gross tonnage.

Beijing has poured more than $90 billion in subsidies into its shipbuilders to secure this advantage—not just in trade, but in **dual-use capability**. In a crisis, those same yards can shift from cargo ships to naval frigates almost overnight. Such scale and speed aren't just commercial, they're central to national security.

Ports follow the ships. Beijing or its state firms now hold stakes in roughly 100 harbors from Piraeus in Greece to Piraí in Brazil (see Exhibit 16: global port encirclement). The largest single operator isn't even a state firm. CK Hutchison, a Hong Kong–based private company, controls 30 ports globally, giving Beijing influence with commercial cover.[76]

In November 2024, COSCO, a state-owned Chinese conglomerate, opened Peru's deep-water Chancay terminal, a $1.3 billion facility funded largely by China.[77] The port offers China a direct Atlantic–Pacific link that bypasses the Panama Canal, where CK Hutchison already controls terminals at both ends: the Port of Balboa on the Pacific side and the Port of Cristobal on the Atlantic side. China has **positioned itself on both sides of the hemisphere's critical choke point** and plants Chinese logistics just two hours from Lima.

Exhibit 16: Global Port Encirclement

China Has Built Global Dominance over Ports

Deep-sea container ports outside of mainland China and Hong Kong where Chinese companies are involved

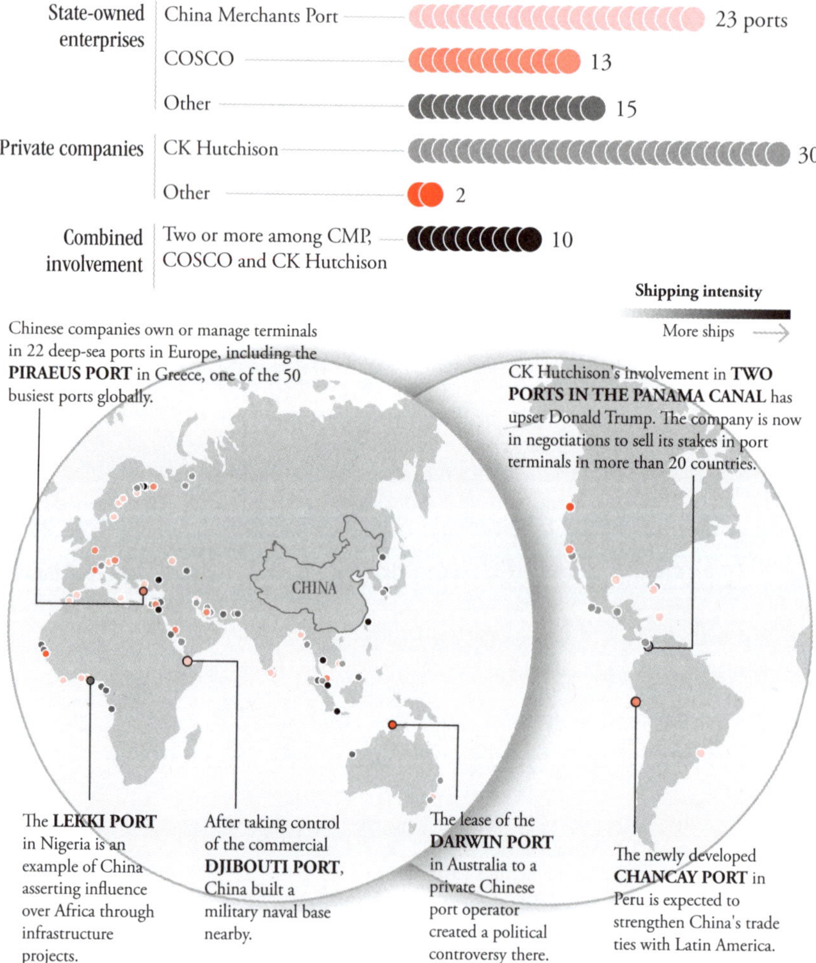

Sources: Analysis by Isaac Kardon, Carnegie Endowment for International Peace; Natural Earth; IMF Global Commercial Shipping Traffic Density (Jan. 2015–Feb. 2021)

Note: Chinese involvement in ports may include an ownership stake in a port or a terminal or concessions to operate it. Involvement may include one or more terminals and is as of Oct. 6. China Merchants Port includes interests held through Terminal Link, a joint venture with the French company CMA CGM.

Nominally, these are commercial assets. But every port is dual-purpose. In Sri Lanka, a default on BRI loans forced a 99-year lease of Hambantota Port to China.[78] Each of these sites can host the People's Liberation Army (PLA) Navy with 48 hours' notice.

A canal across Nicaragua, long dismissed as a fantasy, is back on the table as Managua courts Beijing and distances itself from Taiwan.[79] Should it break ground, China would hold a second trans-isthmus choke point. This one even closer to the US Gulf coast.

Piece by piece, Beijing is building not just ships or ports. It is building control over maritime logistics.

Crane in the Yard, Eye in the Hold

Washington's security agencies recently found unauthorized data-links buried inside Chinese-made ship-to-shore cranes at US ports.[80] Hardware capable of mapping cargo movements in real time. Ten US harbors with Chinese investment already offer what the Council on Foreign Relations calls "physical potential for naval use." The infrastructure is in place; intent can shift overnight.[81]

INTELLIGENCE CHANNELS: WIRING THE WORLD FOR DATA

Undersea fiber is the **hidden bloodstream of global commerce**, carrying 99 percent of intercontinental traffic and an estimated $22 trillion in financial transfers every workday.[82] The entire system is built, owned, operated, and maintained by the private sector.

A vast majority of it is installed by just a handful of firms. As of 2021, US-based SubCom, France's Alcatel Submarine Networks, and Japan's Nippon Electric Company held a combined 87 percent share.[83] China's HMN Tech holds another 11 percent, and is expanding. Chinese firms now manufacture, install, or maintain a growing share of those cables and supply core telecom gear to more than 100 countries.

Ownership matters because whoever builds and repairs the cables holds the keys to their security.

Sabotage is no longer hypothetical. Two Baltic cables were damaged in late 2024, with suspicion falling on an anchor dragged by a Chinese vessel.[84] In April 2025, Taiwan charged a Chinese ship captain with intentionally damaging undersea cables off its coast, following a spike in malfunctions. Five incidents were reported in the first half of 2025 alone.[85]

US officials are now warning of a subtler risk: Chinese state-controlled repair companies operating in the Pacific. One, Shanghai-based S.B. Submarine Systems has been accused of hiding its vessels' locations from radio and satellite tracking, behavior that defies easy explanation.[86]

China's capabilities are advancing, too. A new Chinese-built submersible tool can cut armored fiber at 4,000 meters, twice the depth of most cables today.[87] Place that capability near Guam, and an entire theater command goes dark.

A senior US cyber-diplomat put it bluntly: *"If the supplier answers to an authoritarian state, the cable's security is only as strong as that state's intentions."*

ACCESS LEVERS: DIPLOMACY, DEBT, AND VOTES

The physical network is reinforced by political leverage. Loans tied to BRI projects often come with a quiet clause: alignment with Beijing in multilateral forums and access to the raw materials that power its factories. At the 2024 Forum on China-Africa Cooperation, 53 of 55 African states pledged support for China's "reunification" with Taiwan; at least 49 had active Chinese loans.[88]

Over the last two decades, China's direct loans and trade credits grew from nearly zero to $1.6 trillion by 2018, making it the largest bilateral creditor in history.[89] Today, more than 160 countries owe China money or run trade deficits with it. Only a handful—countries like Australia, Brazil, and Saudi Arabia—escape this web from which China secures vital raw inputs for its industrial machine (see Exhibit 17: China's resource dependencies[90]).

Exhibit 17: China's Trade Deficit: Top 10 Countries

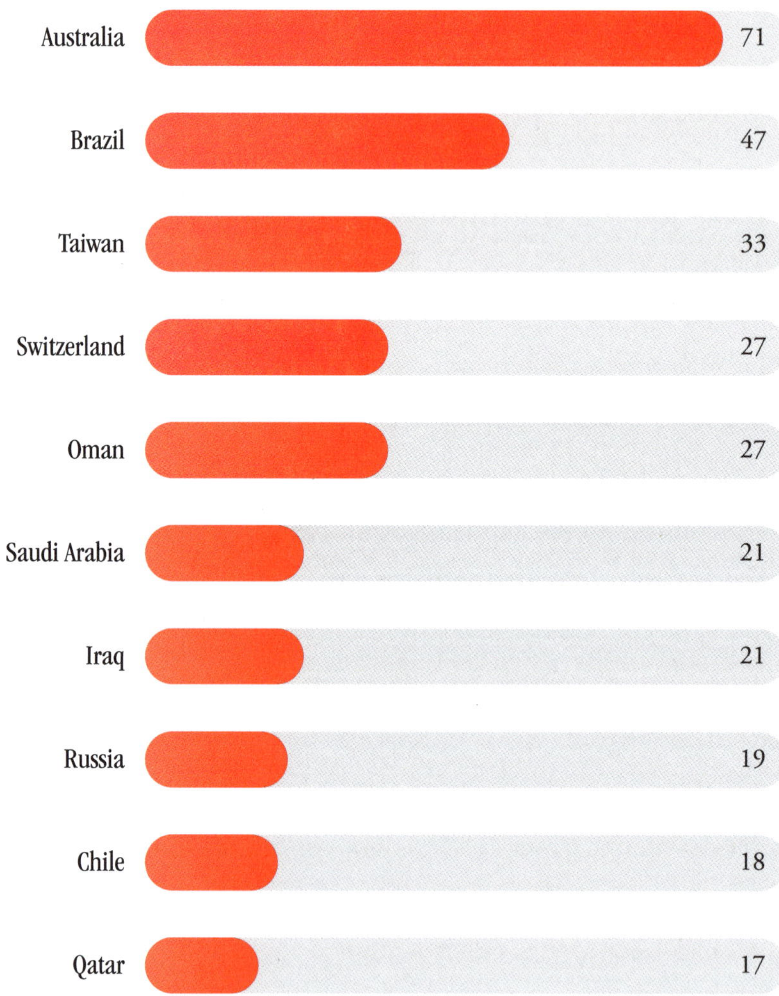

Source: The Observatory of Economic Complexity (OEC)

The dependencies are existential. Australian iron ore powers steel mills. Middle Eastern crude runs factories and warships. Brazilian soybeans feed 1.4 billion people. Chilean copper enables China's EV and renewable ambitions. China cannot produce these domestically at the scale required. So, it converts resource dependence into supplier dependence through trade volumes so massive that commodity exporters cannot afford to lose Chinese demand.

Beijing translates that financial weight into **exclusive access.** One loan, one contract, one vote at a time. In Congo, $6 billion in infrastructure bought control over key cobalt mines.[91] In Saudi Arabia, long-term oil contracts purchase more than crude. They mute dissent in OPEC and G20 corridors.

Pushback is real. Sri Lanka, Pakistan, and Bangladesh have challenged the harsh terms. But Beijing adjusts. It forgave $610 million in African debt in 2021 and waived interest on loans to 33 countries in 2024, preserving influence while easing friction.[92] The asymmetry holds: China can refinance, restructure, or repossess. Its partners cannot.

In Latin America (LATAM), once a US-dominated sphere, China became the largest extra-regional trading partner by 2023, overturning decades of American economic leadership (see Exhibit 18: LATAM encirclement[93]). With that trade came something more potent: voting power in international forums, seats at multilateral lending institutions, and growing regulatory influence that increasingly mirrors Beijing's preferences.

Exhibit 18: Latin America's Encirclement: How the Tide Turned

Largest extraregional trading partners, by total value of goods traded

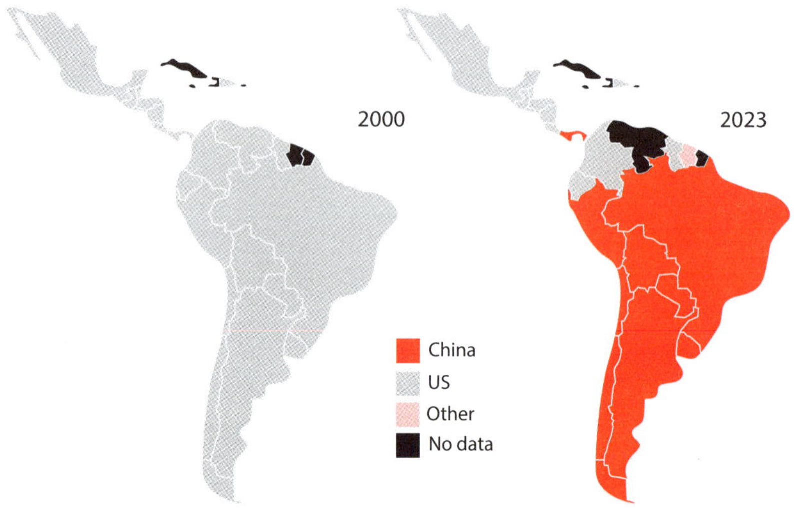

Note: No 2023 data for Venezuela.
Sources: United Nations Comtrade Database

Chinese Loans and Resulting Debt Trap, 2023

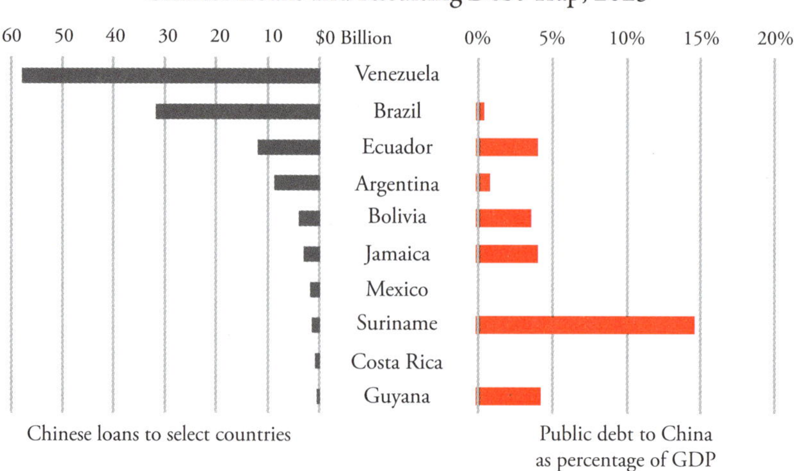

Note: No debt data available for Costa Rica and Venezuela.
Sources: Inter-American Dialogue (loans); Boston University Global Development Policy Center (debt)

Washington and its allies have countered with diplomatic bursts—joint naval drills in the Philippines, infrastructure financing in Africa—but nothing yet rivals the long-game coherence of China's playbook. **Flow control is no longer just about ships and cables.** It's about who holds the pen on the loan that decides whose cargo moves first.

MY TAKE FOR BUSINESS LEADERS

One must give President Xi credit: He has imagined and constructed a China-owned web of logistics, shipping lanes, energy corridors, and data flows that stretch across the Pacific and into nearly 150 countries. He has given this system **top priority and driven it personally**, ensuring that the companies he built cannot be easily interrupted by the West.

With routes secured, markets linked, and a supply of raw materials from exporters like Australia and Brazil, **China is increasingly self-contained.** The asymmetry is stark: If Xi cannot get advanced technologies, he falls short of surpassing the US. But if America cannot secure the rare earths and magnets essential to modern industry, it risks being strangled at the source.

This reality carries profound implications for business leaders. The combination of globally dominant companies and total control of market routes, including the arteries of data and intelligence, creates risks that should feel daunting, even frightening, for non-Chinese firms. Which is why these five imperatives demand your attention:

1. **Audit your exposure.** Map every point in your supply chain—physical and digital—where Chinese control could slow, redirect, or surveil your flow. Assume those levers will be pulled when the stakes are high enough.
2. **Diversify routes and partners.** Redundancy is no longer a luxury; it is survival. Secure alternative ports, carriers, and telecom backbones outside Beijing's network.
3. **Watch the data layer.** Subsea cable *"accidents"* that once seemed random may now be pressure tests. Build latency-tolerant systems and localize critical workloads.
4. **Engage, but ring-fence.** A full withdrawal may be neither realistic nor necessary. Protect core technologies and know-how while containing exposure.
5. **Factor speed into strategy.** China's advantage is not only scale but velocity—of financing, of construction, of adaptation. Unless your governance and investment processes match that tempo, you will always be reacting instead of leading.

Ports, cables, debts, and deals—each secures China's grip on the arteries of global commerce. Stay alert. Stay mobile. Be aware of the arteries you depend on. In your next negotiation, remember the phrase *"What's mine is mine; what's yours is negotiable."* Know which is which before you sit down.

Chapter 5

Conscripting Technology: The Rise of China's Military Machine

I am not a military strategist. I don't claim expertise in warfare. But I have spent years listening to those who are. Combining their knowledge with my own tracking of facts, patterns, and capabilities, I have no doubt that **China is preparing for war**. That preparation is a major part of President Xi's domination strategy.

China has already built global companies and seized control of the routes that connect them to markets. With that foundation laid, it is channeling its trade surpluses into advanced technology and military power.

Where does that technology come from? In Chapter 3, we saw how China conscripted Western innovation through forced technology transfers and commercial partnerships. Apple's precision manufacturing. Tesla's EV systems. Huawei's telecom infrastructure. All built on knowledge extracted from America and its allies.

Now that technology is being **weaponized**. The same precision manufacturing that produces smartphones now produces guidance systems for hypersonic missiles. The same battery technology that powers electric vehicles now powers naval vessels. The same AI developed for autonomous driving now directs military drones and surveillance networks. This is a **military-civil fusion**: commercial innovation **conscripted** and converted into military capability.

Beijing presents this as self-defense. Yet the speed, scale, and rehearsal of its forces suggest readiness to strike if necessary. China's military buildup is no longer subtle (see Exhibit 19: military encirclement[94]). Just look, and you will see pieces moving on the game board.

Exhibit 19: China's Military Encirclement

Source: Foundation for Defense of Democracies, "Mapping the Expansion of China's Global Military Footprint"

The map reveals China's methodical construction of a global military network. Forward bases across Asia, Africa, and Latin America that extend the People's Liberation Army (PLA) power projection thousands of miles from home. Add the Russia–North Korea alliance, which began in 2014 and intensified dramatically after the 2022 Ukraine invasion, and the threat geometry becomes unprecedented.

Today, this trilateral axis can strike the American mainland in approximately 30 minutes via North Korean intercontinental ballistic missiles (ICBMs), with US missile defenses receiving alert just 20 seconds after launch and deploying interceptors around 11 minutes later, leaving critical gaps that could allow missiles to slip through.[95] The global reach on this map, plus coordinated nuclear capability from three adversaries, represents a threat America has never confronted.

Not just ships and missiles, but the erection of warehouses, silos, and contingency stockpiles. The country is quietly amassing defense-linked commodities like oil and gas—but also wheat, maize, and soybeans, enough to feed its 400 million pigs. As *The Financial Times* reported, this isn't preparation for peaceful coexistence. It's preparation for a prolonged struggle.[96]

President Xi has taken what his predecessors only theorized and made it concrete. The military buildup that began as a hedge against Western aggression has now transformed into a revved-up, tech-fueled machine designed to deter, disrupt, and dominate. Xi denies any aggressive intent, but the capabilities being developed and deployed tell a verifiable story.

HARD POWER, GLOBAL REACH

The PLA is no longer a regional force. It is being rebuilt into a global power projection system.

China's provocations are no longer limited to Taiwan. Chinese warships and aircraft have challenged freedom of navigation from the East China Sea to Australia's northern coast, harassed Canadian and US patrol planes, and rammed vessels in contested waters across the Pacific. According to the Pentagon, there were at least 180 dangerous air intercepts by China against US aircraft in just two years.[97]

In December 2024, a Department of Defense report revealed that China had expanded its nuclear arsenal by over 100 warheads in a single year—now approaching 600, with projections of 1,000 by 2030.[98] Its defense spending, officially around $220 billion, is estimated to actually be $330–450 billion. That's nearly **double** what it was just 11 years ago, making it the **second-largest defense budget in the world**, behind only the US at approximately **$850 billion**.[99] Much of this funding has gone to:

- Developing ICBMs capable of reaching the US
- Building the world's largest navy (370-plus ships, surpassing America's 290)[100]
- Leading the world in hypersonic missile development

A NAVY-FIRST, GLOBALLY DEPLOYED FORCE

Naval power has become the centerpiece of China's military ambitions. The PLA Navy (PLAN) is now the world's largest by ship count. But this isn't just about numbers. China is investing in blue-water capabilities—aircraft carriers, long-range submarines, and amphibious assault ships—built not for coastal defense, but for global deployment.

China's naval exercises now span the Pacific, Indian Ocean, and increasingly, the Atlantic. It has constructed artificial islands in the South China Sea with military runways and radar installations. It operates intelligence outposts in Djibouti and has scouted base options in Equatorial Guinea and Argentina. Beijing understands a basic principle of sea power: **Control the oceans, and you control the arteries of global trade.**

And these assets aren't confined to China's immediate borders. Through BRI, China has financed and constructed ports with potential dual-use capabilities across Africa, Southeast Asia, and Latin America.

General Laura Richardson of US Southern Command put it bluntly: China is now "on the 20-yard line of our homeland." She cited Peru's Chancay Port, a Chinese-financed project, as a likely PLA logistics hub.[101]

FUELING THE ENGINE: TECHNOLOGY FIRST

The modern battlefield is digital, autonomous, and asymmetric. Xi Jinping and his military planners understand that **future wars will be won not by sheer manpower** or heavy machinery, but by data, drones, and software-defined platforms.

This is why China has made technological dominance a pillar of its military doctrine. In April 2024, Xi announced a complete PLA restructuring to emphasize technology-driven forces. Top generals are replaced frequently, often every nine months, reflecting a culture of ruthlessness and urgency.

Eric Schmidt, former Google CEO, and General Mark Milley, former chairman of the Joint Chiefs, wrote that *"future wars will be dominated by autonomous systems and powerful algorithms."*[102] China is operationalizing that insight.

Drones, AI systems, autonomous vehicles, and battlefield robotics are now central to the PLA's thinking. Here's what that means:

- DJI, the Shenzhen-based drone manufacturer, holds an estimated 70 percent of the global commercial drone market.[103]
- PLA-linked institutions have developed AI tools using open-source US models (e.g., Meta's Llama) and China's own DeepSeek AI.[104]
- China has begun deploying AI tools for noncombat military operations—testing before wider battlefield rollout.[105]

In June 2024, the US Congress passed a bill banning DJI drones for national security reasons. But the underlying problem is broader: China is using the guise of civilian tech to incubate military capabilities.

THE PROXY WAR PLAYBOOK

President Xi may not launch a full war against the US in the near term. But he has already started a proxy war.

China supports and aligns with actors who drain Western military capacity: Russia in Ukraine, Iran and its proxies in the Middle East, and North Korea across East Asia. The Chinese military has joined joint exercises in the Arctic with Russia and hosted observers from 15 nations.

This is deliberate.

Every fire lit by an ally or proxy stretches US resources thinner. Ammunition, logistics, leadership attention, it all becomes a game of overload. The US is forced to fight multiple low-grade wars simultaneously while China consolidates power.

Inventory levels of key munitions are low. The US must support Ukraine, reinforce Israel, prepare for Taiwan, and deter Iranian expansion, all at once. And this suits China's strategy.

RECRUITING THE FUTURE

China is in a global recruiting frenzy for high-tech scientists and engineers. It aggressively seeks foreign expertise in aerospace, semiconductors, quantum computing, and AI. Programs like the Thousand Talents Plan have openly offered top researchers generous incentives to relocate or collaborate, often without transparency around end use.[106]

Military-civil fusion, a doctrine embedded in China's national strategy, blurs the line between civilian research and military development. That means any partnership, even one focused on climate or health, can become a channel for technology transfer.

Expect this to become a central issue in any negotiation with China. Technology access will be their key ask.

MY TAKE FOR BUSINESS LEADERS

One cannot ignore the **clouds of war**. And they are intensifying every day. Xi's military buildup is no longer hidden; it is visible in trade flows, stockpiles, weapons tests, and proxy alignments. His actions make clear that China is preparing not just for a clash, but for a long, technology-led contest of power.

Even if you are not in the defense sector, this reshaping of the landscape will reach your boardroom. Why? Because the very items that dominate commercial markets—drones, chips, rare earths, AI platforms—are the same ones that decide military advantage. When one country holds a dominant share in both, the line between commerce and conflict disappears.

Here is what that means for you:

1. **Technology is now geopolitical.** If your business touches AI, semiconductors, drones, quantum computing, biotech, or

advanced materials, assume you are operating in a contested space. These are not just commercial assets; they are national security priorities. Expect regulations, export controls, and international scrutiny to intensify.

2. **Dual-use is the new reality.** Many technologies now serve both civilian and military purposes. Drones, chips, and software platforms. Collaborations once seen as benign may now trigger regulatory risk. Know how your innovations could be weaponized and give weight to national security.
3. **Supply chains are potential battlefields.** China's military strategy is intertwined with its industrial base. If you rely on Chinese suppliers in aerospace, electronics, robotics, or critical minerals, you may already be exposed to strategic vulnerabilities. Diversification and data security are no longer optional.
4. **Talent is a national asset.** China has intensified foreign talent recruitment far beyond anything seen in the past decade. Engineers and scientists are being recruited globally, sometimes covertly with offers that exceed Western compensation by two or three times. Scrutinize who has access to your R&D and where your people go after they leave. The line between civilian and military knowledge transfer is thin and fading.
5. **Investment due diligence must evolve.** If you're funding or partnering with firms in sensitive sectors, understand who else

is involved, especially if Chinese capital or joint ventures are in play. What looks like innovation today could become export-controlled or politically radioactive tomorrow. And don't let data and know-how leak in the name of joint innovation.

6. **Your long-term planning horizon just got shorter.** The assumption of peace has underwritten global business for decades. That's changing. Scenario planning should now include geopolitical rupture, not just economic cycles. War by proxy, cyber disruption, or open conflict in Asia could affect your markets, pricing, and capital flows overnight.

Does that create an alarm in your mind? It should. The **encirclement** is close to complete, and Xi is forcing the West to react. The only question is if, and who, pulls the switch first.

Chapter 6

Xi's War Without Firing a Shot

The previous chapters mapped the CCP's hard-power playbook: dominant companies, total control of global logistics, and military buildup. But there is a fourth pillar—less visible, more insidious. It rests on two quiet but potent weapons: **distraction** and **distortion**.

President Xi lights fires across the globe to stretch the West's focus thin—**distraction**. At the same time, his Party wages a psychological campaign to weaken democratic confidence and reshape the narrative of power—**distortion**. Without firing a shot, China chips away at unity, clarity, and resolve. This is the **soft battlefield**. And it is central to the CCP's strategy.

The **psychological campaign** is working. CEOs from Brazil to India to Japan to America tell me the same thing: China is too far ahead to catch. That defeatism is Beijing's goal.

DISTRACTION: LIGHTING FIRES ACROSS THE MAP

Stand back from the daily headlines, and you will see the pattern clearly. Beijing keeps a single objective in mind—tilt the global board in its favor—yet it pursues that aim by igniting small, overlapping crises that force Washington and its partners to chase every spark.

- **Europe:** China buys discounted Russian oil, indirectly fueling Moscow's war machine. Meanwhile, US aid to Ukraine, exceeding $100 billion,[107] dwarfs contributions from allies, crowding out other American priorities (see Exhibit 20: diverting American resources).
- **Middle East:** China's embrace of Iran gave Hamas political cover and access to money and training, while Beijing deepened its ties with Tehran by supplying missile components and buying nearly all of its sanctioned oil. The October 2023 assault on Israel set off a war that ground on for two years, absorbing US military and diplomatic bandwidth just as China pressed its ambitions in the Indo-Pacific. This is distraction by design.
- **Indo-Pacific:** Chinese coast guard "fishing boats" ram Philippine resupply ships. PLA Air Force jets buzz Taiwan. Live-fire drills erupt near the disputed Senkaku Islands administered by Japan. Each flare-up forces the US to react.

Exhibit 20: Diverting the American Leadership's Time and Resources

Ukraine Towers over Other Recipients of US Aid

Aid committed to the government of Ukraine (military, financial, and humanitarian) for fiscal year 2022–24 compared with aid to top recipients for fiscal year 2020–22 (the most recent three years available)

Note: Data for Ukraine and data for comparison countries are from different sources, and the categories included could differ. Data for Ukraine comes from the Kiel Institute for the World Economy because the data source used for comparison countries (foreignassistance.gov) does not currently include all aid to Ukraine for recent years.
Source: Council on Foreign Relations

US Aid to Ukraine Far Exceeds That from Other Countries

Bilateral aid commitments from the top 20 donor countries and from European Union (EU) institutions as of June 30, 2024

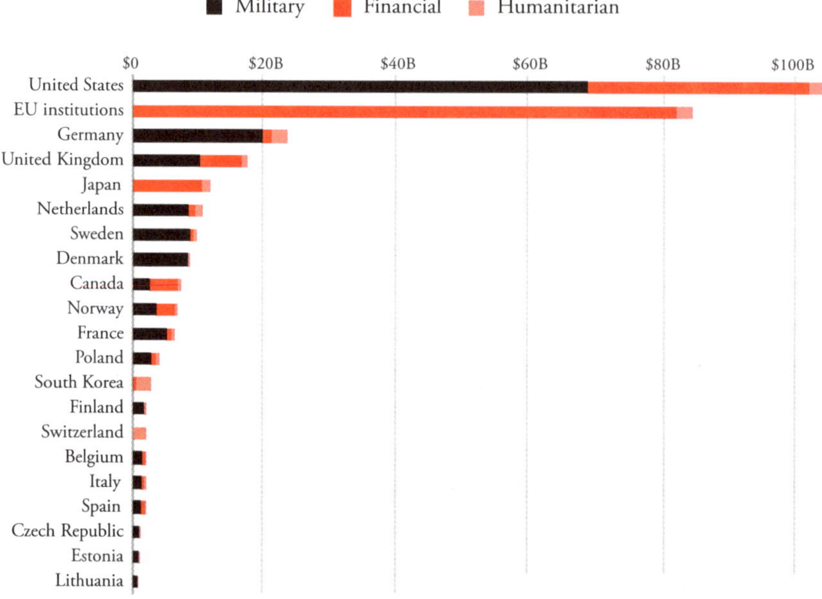

Note: Data source includes Australia, China, Iceland, India, New Zealand, Norway, South Korea, Switzerland, Taiwan, Turkey, EU member states, and members of the Group of Seven (G7).
Source: Council on Foreign Relations

These fires are **cheap to light and costly to extinguish**. They stretch American capacity and sow partisan rifts at home. This is not chaos. It is calculus.

Beijing's second tactic within this distraction playbook is a classic **divide-and-conquer play**: to split the Western alliance, especially by driving wedges between Europe and the US:

- **Trade Seduction:** The stalled EU-China Comprehensive Agreement on Investment nearly gave European firms preferential access to Chinese markets. Only last-minute US pressure and China's Xinjiang sanctions froze the deal. Today, with rising US tariff threats, up to 50 percent on some sectors, Europe is again weighing Chinese overtures more carefully. A July 2025 EU-China summit, while inconclusive, marked a shift. Several capitals now see Chinese investment as a hedge against US trade uncertainty.

- **Rare Earth Diplomacy:** June 2025 saw Beijing unveil a *"green channel"* for fast-tracking magnet exports[108]—*to Europe only*. The subtext: Stay close to Washington, and that tap can close overnight.
- **Carrot-and-Stick Tariffs:** President Xi's envoys now float "proactive" tariff cuts on seafood, telecom gear, and farm goods—sweeteners tailored to swing specific EU votes. This comes as some EU leaders grow more open to Chinese capital, particularly in renewables and infrastructure, as a counterbalance to American pressure.
- **Industrial Entrapment:** Germany's auto giants spent decades helping build China's car industry; now the teacher is outcompeted and heavily dependent on the pupil. With Trump's tariffs on European cars and the loss of Russian gas, Berlin faces a stark dilemma: Stay aligned with Beijing or risk industrial decline and geopolitical isolation.

Meanwhile, China is lighting a quieter fire. One that doesn't make headlines but strikes at the heart of America's global reach.

It is working methodically to **shift the world's energy flows and financial plumbing** away from the dollar and toward the RMB:

- **Yuan-priced oil:** Discussions with Saudi Crown Prince Mohammed bin Salman over RMB settlements are real. Adding yuan-denominated futures to Aramco's benchmarks would hard-wire China into the world's oil ledger and thin America's financial armor.
- **Pipeline politics:** From Russia's Siberian wells to ports in the Gulf of Tonkin, Beijing funds every hose that can bypass a US naval choke point. The goal is to make oil and gas flows shock-resistant and politically steerable.
- **Resource triage:** Once secured, these energy flows are rerouted to favor whichever domestic industry Beijing wants to scale. In wartime, they can be weaponized.

But energy is just one lever. The broader ambition is to weaken the US-created financial architecture and eventually displace the dollar itself. The dollar's share of global reserves has fallen from 71 percent to 58 percent, while nontraditional currencies have surged from 2 percent to 11 percent, with China's renminbi capturing a significant and symbolically powerful share (see Exhibit 21: USD as global currency[109]).

Exhibit 21: Evolution of USD as Global Currency

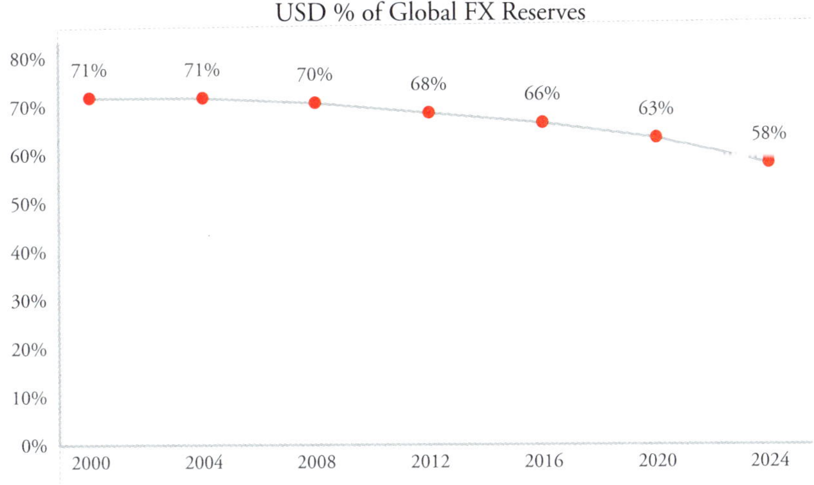

Source: ING, "DE-Dollarisation: More BRICS in the Wall"

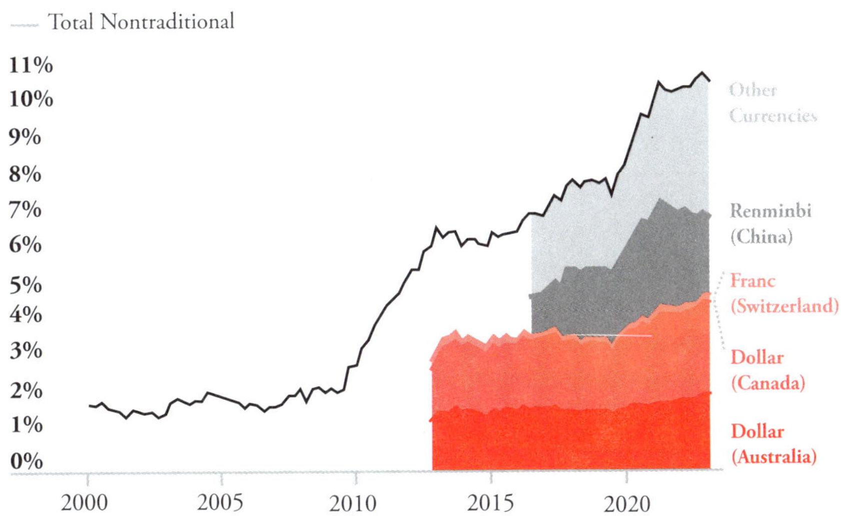

Source: Brookings, "The Changing Role of the US Dollar"

Even world leaders are echoing the line: *"The world needs to find a way that our trade relations don't have to pass through the dollar,"* Brazil's President Lula declared at the BRICS summit in Rio.[110]

The CCP is pushing hard to make RMB the default currency in more and more corners of global trade. The pitch to partner countries: Settle deals in yuan and sidestep the Western system entirely. The effort is already visible in agriculture and energy, with food-for-yuan transactions rising alongside oil-for-yuan contracts.

A breakthrough came when China struck a deal with Saudi Arabia to begin importing energy—and potentially settling it—in yuan. Moscow and Tehran have already shifted. And Beijing is backing it all with real financial infrastructure.

- **CIPS over SWIFT:** China's Cross-Border Interbank Payment System (CIPS) is its alternative to SWIFT. It doesn't yet have a 24/7 global reach, but it's maturing fast.
- **Digital tools:** China's e-CNY pilot is laying the groundwork for programmable cross-border settlements that could one day escape all Western oversight.

The numbers are still small, but the direction is clear. RMB's share of global payments hovered around 2 percent for much of the late 2010s before rising to roughly 3–4 percent by late 2023, while its share of global trade finance climbed from under 2 percent in early 2022 to about 4.5 percent in 2023.[111] **Propaganda has inflated the narrative**, but the strategic implications are real.

In my experience, the RMB is nowhere near replacing the dollar. But complacency would be foolish. This is not just monetary experimentation; it is a soft war for financial sovereignty.

DISTORTION: WEAPONIZING PERCEPTION AND INFLUENCE

Distraction spreads America thin. But distortion reshapes how the world sees itself, and China. What makes the CCP dangerous here is not one tactic but a **masterful blend**: polished propaganda, relentless lobbying, soft infiltration of universities and think tanks, and hard-edged bullying that puts Washington permanently on the defensive. Even the American public, fed a steady stream of China's showcase narratives, can slip into **quiet awe** at its scale and speed.

The CCP has embraced what it calls cognitive domain operations. The aim is to erode self-confidence in democracy, amplify China's inevitability, and make resistance seem futile.

The Message: Democracy Is Dysfunctional, Autocracy Delivers

Beijing's psychological campaign rests on a central belief: that democracies are weak, fractured, and incapable of long-term strategy. And they are determined to make the world believe it too. The CCP's propaganda machine routinely asserts that America's democratic process—frequent elections, institutional checks, divided governance—makes strategic planning impossible.

"America can't make decisions," they argue. *"It changes leadership every four years. Its presidents are boxed in by political gridlock."*

This messaging isn't confined to Chinese media. It travels through diplomats, think tanks, financial elites, and increasingly, American and European public discourse. It's seeded into conversations, op-eds, expert panels, and social media.

The repetition works. Business leaders begin to wonder if the West can still execute. Journalists echo China's talking points. A slow drip of doubt erodes the confidence that underpins democratic resilience.

Coercion and Compliance

The Party does more than broadcast ideas. It enforces them. Anyone perceived as crossing the line can face retribution.

When Elon Musk cut Tesla prices in China in 2023, regulators pushed back. Soon after, Musk made a public pledge to uphold China's "core socialist values." The signal was unmistakable.

During President Xi's 2023 visit to San Francisco, pro-democracy protestors were attacked by private security guards hired by Chinese diplomats. The message: Dissent will be punished.

That same pattern holds globally. Australia criticized China's handling of COVID-19. Within weeks, Beijing cut $25 billion in coal, wine, and other imports.[112] Norway, Lithuania, and others have been hit with retaliatory trade bans after voicing support for Taiwan or human rights.

The goal is to instill caution. To make leaders, executives, and institutions self-censor before ever taking a stand.

Elite Capture and Soft Infiltration

Psychological warfare needs messengers. So, Beijing cultivates them.

Former French Prime Minister Jean-Pierre Raffarin now sits on Chinese state-backed boards, lending global legitimacy to Beijing's ambitions. Between 2013 and 2019, Harvard received nearly $100 million in Chinese-linked donations.[113] Research labs across the US quietly welcomed Chinese scholars, some tied to military-adjacent programs.

In 2024, Georgia Tech severed ties with the Shenzhen Institute after learning it was involved in dual-use research. That same year, Linda Sun—an aide to two New York governors—was indicted for allegedly acting as a covert Chinese agent. She blocked Taiwan meetings, altered diplomatic language, and reshaped US messaging to China's liking from the inside.

The pattern is subtle but consistent: Cultivate elites, embed influence, and steer the conversation without ever raising a flag.

As Congressman John Moolenaar put it: *"The CCP isn't simply way over there. They are on our shores and working to subvert the American experience."*

Repeating the Narrative Until It Sticks

The CCP's talking points are remarkably consistent:

- America is declining.
- China's rise is inevitable.
- Resistance is futile; accommodation is wise.

These ideas show up in boardrooms, editorial pages, and even sports arenas. At a Mets game in 2022, a video praised the CCP while fans wore hats with Chinese flags, sponsored by a known propaganda outfit. In April 2025, American influencer IShowSpeed, with over 120 million followers, spent 10 days in China.[114] His viral videos, marveling at bullet trains and electric cars, handed Beijing a global soft-power win.

The message isn't limited to pop culture. Elon Musk, Tim Cook, and Jamie Dimon have all made high-profile visits to China. The receptions are grand. The message back home is implicit: China is the future. Play ball or get left behind.

Every channel—media, commerce, diplomacy—becomes a theater for psychological warfare.

Service Firms in the Crosshairs

Even service firms that once considered themselves immune—consulting, law, audit, due diligence—are now squarely in the crosshairs. This is not limited to physical supply chains anymore. It's about **know-how**: models, data, decision logic, and intellectual property.

The CEO of one of the world's largest consulting firms personally told me that the CCP demanded the list of their global customers and certain intellectual property as the price of their staying.

This reality has led to self-censorship among global knowledge firms. KPMG and Deloitte now instruct staff to use burner phones, even in Hong Kong. Ratings agencies like Moody's and Fitch are under quiet but intensifying pressure: denied access to critical data, facing threats if they overstep.

In July 2025, BlackRock went further—banning the use of company laptops and remote access via virtual private networks (VPNs) during personal travel in China, cutting employees off from its network entirely. Wells Fargo followed suit, suspending all work travel after one of its senior bankers was barred from leaving the country.

Even the most security-conscious firms now operate on the assumption that no business is safe.

Weaponizing Global Institutions

China now exerts influence inside the UN, IMF, World Bank, and WTO—not through consensus, but through leverage. Many BRI countries vote with China in multilateral forums. That influence helps Beijing shape global standards in AI, 5G, and EVs.

This isn't accidental. China's 2021 plan, China Standards 2035, laid out a blueprint to dominate standard-setting bodies.[115] In 2024, its Ministry of Industry and Information Technology issued global work plans to guide EV and green-tech standards.

A former tech CEO put it bluntly: *"If you're not in the room setting the standard, you're not in the market."*

The Power of the Lie

The most potent tool in China's psychological warfare is deceit. The CCP agrees to terms, then ignores them. It makes commitments, then breaks them. When challenged, it resets the narrative and repeats the pattern.

Take the WTO. Nearly 20 years after joining, China has failed to honor core promises made at the start: fair trade, open markets, and IP protection (see Exhibit 22: failed WTO commitments[116]). Yet it continues to claim full compliance. That's intentional manipulation.

Exhibit 22: China's Failed WTO Commitments

Chinese WTO Commitment	Has China Lived Up to the Commitment?
Embracing open, market-oriented policies	No
Embracing national treatment—treating foreign firms the same as domestic ones	No
SOEs shrinking as a share of the economy, especially in technology industries	No
SOEs making purchases based on commercial considerations	No
Curtailing extensive industrial subsidization	No
Providing timely and transparent notification of subsidies	No
Curtailing forced technology transfer, including through coerced joint ventures	No
IP theft and violations being significantly reduced	No

Technology standards developed transparently according to WTO Technical Barriers to Trade principles	No
Competition and antimonopoly policies applied on nondiscriminatory terms	No
Joining the Government Procurement Agreement	No
Information and communications technology and telecommunications market opening to foreign producers	No
Foreign film distribution being liberalized	No
Foreign banks enjoying genuine national treatment and market access	No
Responsible and nonretaliatory use of trade remedies	No

Source: Information Technology and Innovation Foundation, "The Continuing Gap Between China's WTO Commitments and Its Practices"

The deeper failure, however, lies in Washington. America let those broken promises slide. By refusing to enforce China's commitments, it normalized the deception. Over time, the effect is corrosive: Leaders stop pushing back, markets adjust to the unfair rules, and learned helplessness sets in.

Inside China: Surveillance as a Way of Life

Inside China, the psychological warfare is constant and total. Surveillance is omnipresent. A former US cabinet secretary once told me that during diplomatic visits, they would stage conversations in cars, knowing the driver was reporting directly to the Party. The purpose? To manage what Beijing overheard.

Phones, computers, street cameras, facial recognition—everything feeds the CCP's control system. The Great Firewall censor's information. The social credit system punishes behavior. There are 626 million surveillance cameras in China, the highest in the world, nearly one for every two people.

And this surveillance extends to foreign businesses. A CCP person or cell exists in almost every company or board. Legal protections akin to the US system do not apply. China's data and national security laws are vague by design. Authorities can enter offices, seize files, detain staff, and freeze operations at will.

In 2023 alone, Bain Consulting, Capvision (an expert network group), and Mintz (a due diligence firm) were raided. Firms are targeted without warning, and executives are detained. You do not operate in a predictable, rules-based environment.

Disloyalty is punished without warning. A prominent economist in China disappeared after questioning Party policy on WeChat. Members of the CCP vanish when their statements fall short of total allegiance.

MY TAKE FOR BUSINESS LEADERS

Distraction and distortion are not abstract threats. They reshape markets, alliances, and decision-making environments. If you run a global business, here's what you must consider:

1. **Guard your mental perimeter:** Doubt is contagious. Audit what you've come to believe and why. Is China's rise inevitable? Or is that the story you have been sold?
2. **Know what's being bought:** Market access in China is never free. Your silence, your brand, and your legitimacy are the price.
3. **Understand soft coercion:** China won't sue you. It will stall permits, vanish demand, or revoke deals. Be ready.
4. **Defend your institution's integrity:** Universities, think tanks, and startups are influence targets. Go deep to vet funding, partnerships, and affiliations.
5. **Don't outsource your narrative:** Know the story you're part of. Tell your own, or China will tell it for you.

President Xi is fighting a war without firing a shot. But the battlefield is real, and your business may already be on it. Stay alert. Stay independent. And don't mistake silence for neutrality.

Chapter 7

Assessment of Xi's Strategy: Strengths and Fault Lines

In the chapters before, we saw the machinery of President Xi's modus operandi. His plan of economic and logistical encirclement, digital infiltration, narrative distortion, and alliance disruption is in motion. It is disciplined, fast, and unopposed. And it is backed by a military engine that stays just below the redline.

It is brilliant and meticulously executed with precision and patience, creating a system that is dangerous for the West. The strategy is not improvised; it is deliberate, coordinated, and relentless.

And here is what makes it especially dangerous: It is **invisible to the citizens of the world**. Americans, Europeans, and citizens across democracies are mesmerized by inexpensive, high-quality goods that their local industries cannot produce. Leaders, politicians, and the press have paid little attention because economies have been expanding.

Post-COVID-19 fiscal investment, booming stock markets, cheap Chinese products—citizens love it. Investors feast on the results.

This brilliant strategy will have a devastating impact on America and other democracies. It was not until China played its first card, threatening to cut off rare earth shipments within a month or a week, that industry leaders finally woke up. That is the weapon for which the Western world doesn't yet have a corresponding response. Until America and its allies find an equally counterbalancing weapon, they remain bound by the actions of one man, President Xi.

Now, let's step back from the details and assess the system as a whole. What are its real strengths? Where does it fray? And what does it demand from you, the executive, investor, or policymaker, sitting on the other side of the map?

THE STRENGTHS: WHY IT WORKS

President Xi enjoys structural advantages no Western leader can replicate:

- **Unity of Command:** One man, one party, one purpose. He can redirect rare earth exports, forgive African debt, or reroute entire supply chains without a single parliamentary vote.
- **The 90 Percent Model:** Overcapacity at home fuels exports abroad. The surpluses—built through protected markets, global demand, and a deliberately undervalued yuan—fund port-building, tech subsidies, and foreign influence.

- **Globally Dominant Companies:** State-backed firms, scaled at speed, that underprice rivals, absorb foreign know-how, and tilt markets in China's favor.
- **Control of Logistics:** Ports, cables, railways, and data backbones that ensure China's firms can reach global markets while others remain dependent on Chinese arteries.
- **Debt diplomacy** that buys silence in global forums.
- **Psychological warfare** that convinces the world that accommodation is rational and resistance is reckless.
- Together, they give Beijing speed, scale, and—perhaps most dangerously—**an aura of invincibility**.

THE FAULT LINES: WHERE IT FRAYS

But nothing about this system is unbreakable.

- **It depends on hard-currency inflows** from the West. The dollar is still the bloodstream of global trade. Slow that flow, and Beijing must choose between funding its ambitions and keeping domestic calm.
- **Its energy and food lifelines are brittle.** Stockpiles last months. The inputs that keep its factories humming—ore, oil, soy, lithium—still come from outside its control.
- **It lags in critical technology implementation.** China still trails in the execution and scaling of frontier technologies like

extreme-ultraviolet lithography, advanced semiconductors, and the deepest layers of AI. While it publishes prolifically and is advancing in research, turning that into scalable, world-class capability still relies on American and allied know-how, systems integration, and global talent flows. It's catching up, but not there yet.

- **It lacks the institutions of science.** Unlike the US, China does not have the dense network of universities, private labs, public agencies, and venture ecosystems that generate the breakthrough technologies of 2050. Subsidies can build factories; they cannot easily substitute for Stanford, MIT, Bell Labs, or DARPA.
- **Its demographics are destiny.** China is growing old before it grows rich. It has a shrinking workforce, rising pension burden, and no real immigration solution.

MY TAKE: THE CRITICAL MOMENT

Under Trump's leadership, Washington is changing its approach to China. **Don't wait for a leadership change in Beijing.** The system preceded Xi and will survive him. In fact, Xi is now consolidating that system to outlast even his own presence. Ruling more through written directives, loyal commissions, and behind-the-scenes orchestration than through constant appearances. Don't count on an economic slowdown to cool ambition; in authoritarian regimes, scarcity often fuels aggression.

What makes this moment dangerous is its momentum. Success creates more momentum, and Xi has built a machine that compounds its own power dominant companies, secured logistics, a swelling military engine, and relentless propaganda. For now, Xi can afford to wait. His likely strategy under Trump is to buy time, drag out negotiations, pocket small wins, and avoid direct confrontation. If denied Western technology, he simply slows his pace; it does not derail his ambition.

The larger risk lies within China itself. If austerity deepens, if public patience frays, if surveillance no longer keeps discontent at bay, then the CCP's grip could weaken from within. Xi knows this. His guardrails—tight control, propaganda, and military readiness—are designed as much to contain his own people as to deter foreign rivals.

WHERE WE GO NEXT

Part I has shown you China's strategy: the 90 Percent Model, the four pillars of encirclement, and Xi's structural advantages and vulnerabilities.

Part II shifts to America's response. What strengths can the West bring to bear? And why is the tide beginning to turn?

PART II

America's Response

Chapter 8

America's Unmatched Strengths

You now know what China is doing. You have seen the 90 Percent Model in action, the encirclement strategy, the assault on American industry. You have seen how it traps businesses, forcing them into a bind where staying means losing control and leaving means taking a hit.

The natural question follows: **Can America fight back?**

The answer is yes. Unequivocally, yes.

But here is the **hard truth**: Relative to China's coordinated assault, America has not been fighting. Not with the focus, urgency, or coordination this moment demands. The arsenal exists. The weapons are real. But they sit largely unused, underdeployed, waiting for leadership willing to pull the trigger.

This chapter is about those weapons. What America holds. What it can deploy. And why, despite possessing overwhelming power, it has allowed China to gain ground.

Don't Sell America Short

You may have come to believe that China now has the upper hand. That belief, carefully amplified by CCP propaganda, has taken root not just in Beijing but in boardrooms and policy circles across the West. I hear it every day from CEOs, investors, and even national security officials: *"Maybe China is too far ahead." "Maybe we've already lost the initiative."*

Let me be clear: I don't accept that. And I urge you not to either.

Yes, China has moved fast. Yes, it has built industrial scale with ruthless determination. But that should not blind us to the deeper truth: America still controls the most important levers of global power—financial flows, the world's largest market, and the innovation ecosystem that powers the future.

The problem is not capacity. It is not capability. It is activation. The strengths are there. But they have not been coordinated, concentrated, or unleashed with the force the moment demands.

I have spent nearly 60 years advising more than 200 American CEOs across sectors and cycles, from Intel and Honeywell to GE and Pfizer. Many of those relationships have lasted decades. I have watched firsthand how they strategize under pressure and what factors they weigh. From that vantage point, I can tell you: Few leaders today fully grasp the strengths America can still bring to bear.

So, before we talk about what should be done next, we need to take stock of what America still has. It is a rare combination of six pillars that, when used in unison, can counter China's assault and redraw the map of global influence.

THE SIX PILLARS OF AMERICAN POWER

1. Access to the US Market

There is no rival to the American consumer market. Every country wants access. All, including China and its proxies, **salivate for it**. Despite Beijing's rhetoric about self-sufficiency, it has abused the generosity of the American people. American openness has fueled global recoveries, powered industrial revivals, and shaped the rise of entire economies. Japan's auto boom, Taiwan's chip ascent, South Korea's electronics surge—all benefited from privileged access to US buyers.

That openness, however, has long been abused. In the name of global hegemony, successive US presidents permitted almost unrestricted access to the American market. Tariffs were kept low. Enforcement was weak. And China, in particular, exploited this generosity: dumping underpriced exports often at a loss while manipulating currency valuations, using subsidies and transshipments, and misleading consumers into believing its efficiency was real. It wasn't. It was engineered. And it **hollowed out critical industries**.

China cannot replicate the US consumer base. It needs it. Despite claims of self-sufficiency, Beijing's economy would collapse without exports and foreign investment. Its use of proxy countries—Mexico, Vietnam, ASEAN—to maintain trade flows reveals just how deep this dependence runs.

I see this dependence firsthand in my work with companies across the globe. Executives cannot afford to lose US market access. It drives their entire export strategy. Chinese officials constantly probe about tariff scenarios and trade frameworks. The **anxiety behind closed doors contradicts the self-sufficiency rhetoric** in public.

If America insists on balanced trade with its key partners, it pulls a lever more powerful than any single policy. Here's why: Access to the US market has delivered China a cumulative $7 trillion plus in hard cash. Surplus that Beijing is using to fund its military buildup, subsidize the 90 Percent Model, and weaponize technology against American interests. Cutting this surplus would **starve the engine funding China's assault** on the US and its allies. Without it, China's GDP will not overtake the West's anytime soon, if ever.

That's why President Xi keeps traveling the world in search of FDI and export continuity. He knows what's at stake. And so should we.

2. Control of the Global Financial System

Most Americans don't realize that the financial system we take for granted is one of our **most potent weapons**. Every international trade, every major cross-border investment, every currency transaction—it all runs through a system built, governed, and still dominated by the US and its European allies.

China depends on this system. It cannot function at this stage without it. Just as China uses rare earths and other choke points as leverage, America and Europe hold a similar ability over global finance.

The Federal Reserve **anchors** the world's monetary system. The dollar remains the world's reserve currency. SWIFT, dollar-clearing, correspondent banking, derivatives, and regulatory regimes—all tie back to US and European control. That means America and its allies can see money flow. Can influence it. And, if necessary, **can cut it off**.

Behind this lies a vast architecture of intelligence and execution: networks that not only facilitate capital flow but give precise visibility and control 24 hours a day. From pricing foreign exchange to regulating complex derivatives and interest rates, this system underwrites the global economy. It is an American creation, and together with European allies, the **US holds full control** over what to stop, what not to stop, and when to stop it.

China's financial system itself was built using US expertise. For decades, firms like Goldman Sachs helped structure Chinese markets. The architecture and plumbing, quite literally, have **American**

fingerprints all over it. America designed the Chinese system, and Beijing knows Washington can weaponize that knowledge.

The 2022 freezing of Russia's reserves—over $300 billion in bonds, cash, and securities held at central depositories and banks worldwide—demonstrated just how real, and devastating, financial warfare can be.[117] **The weapon is operational.** America and its allies have demonstrated that they can and will use it.

Beijing is aware. During Treasury Secretary Janet Yellen's widely reported 2024 trip to Beijing, credible sources inform me that she made it explicit that the US possesses the financial weapons to impose severe consequences. The message was delivered.

Make no mistake: No country can trade, invest, or wage war without moving money. Either directly or surreptitiously. This is why control of financial flows may become America's most decisive lever.

3. Capital Discipline and Innovation

America uses a simple but powerful logic in capital deployment: Capital must earn returns, absorb risk, and generate future growth. This logic is embedded in every layer of the US economy. Misallocated capital is corrected quickly. Markets punish inefficiency.

That's a stark contrast to China's state-owned enterprises and banks, which pursue scale and market share regardless of cost or return. The Chinese model encourages cash losses underwritten by trade surpluses and currency disparity.

But here's the vulnerability: The 90 Percent Model generates the cash and profit that finance China's inefficient capital deployment. The system works when viewed as "**country as company**," the inefficiency gets hidden in aggregate. But company against company, it doesn't work. If the 90 Percent Model collapses and the cash surplus disappears, the value of America's disciplined capital system will become crystal clear. Without that surplus funding its losses, China's system destroys itself.

In contrast, America's capital markets force efficiency, resilience, and reinvention. The dot-com bust and the 2008 financial crisis were painful, but the system self-corrected. That's a hidden strength. This market-based model disciplines failure, rewards invention, and drives long-term gains.

American firms produce roughly twice as much innovation for the same outlay as their Chinese peers. This edge is not only about invention. It's about **know-how**, the embedded skill of turning ideas into outcomes. The ability to integrate advanced AI, hardware, and software is America's unmatched strength.

Some of America's greatest **hidden assets** are its 40-plus government-funded research labs—Los Alamos, Oak Ridge, Lawrence Livermore, Sandia National Laboratories, Argonne National Laboratory, and Pacific Northwest National Laboratory among them (see Exhibit 23: US research ecosystem[118]).

Exhibit 23: US Federal Research Innovation Ecosystem

Federally Funded Research and Development Centers (FFRDCs)

Public-Private Partnership Model: Government agencies provide funding and strategic direction while universities, nonprofit organizations, and industrial firms manage operations

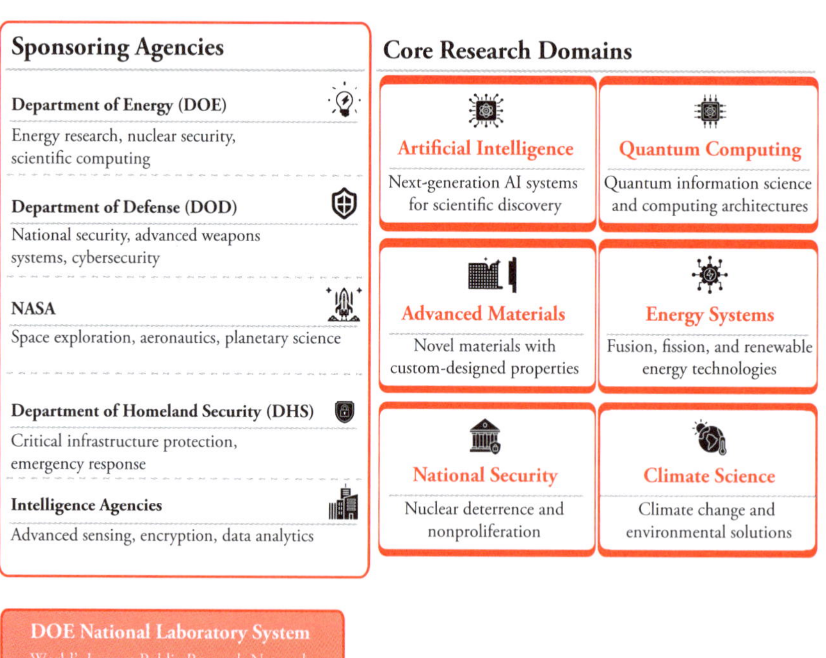

DOE National Laboratory System

World's Largest Public Research Network

17 National Labs | **50** States

Premier National Laboratories

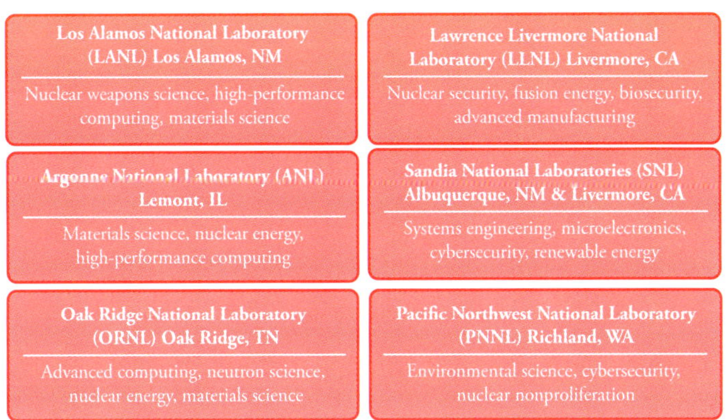

Source: Author's analysis

These institutions are the **envy of President Xi**. They deliver breakthroughs that remain classified for good reason: dual-use technologies that shape both military security and commercial applications. The Department of Energy alone oversees 17 national labs employing over 60,000 scientists and engineers working across six core research domains: artificial intelligence, quantum computing, advanced materials, energy systems, national security, and climate science.

This ecosystem, spanning defense labs, private innovation hubs, and startups born from military R&D, forms the backbone of America's future capability. **China has nothing comparable** in scale, openness, or integration between government and private enterprise.

AI and quantum computing will define the next frontier. Here, America holds a decisive edge. The advanced algorithmic brains in the US are exceptional. A rare **melting pot** of Indians, Americans,

Israelis, Iranians, and Russians. This fusion of talent is uniquely American. And as former Secretary of State Henry Kissinger and Google's Eric Schmidt have warned: **In war, algorithms matter**. America's edge here may well decide the wars of the future.

4. America's Open Social and Political Architecture

The single most underestimated advantage America holds is the openness and vitality of its social and political architecture. Its underpinning is freedom for individual initiative, where one can do anything within the rule of law and cultural norms. This is not a soft asset. It is a hard power multiplier.

In America, individual initiative thrives. Anyone can try. Anyone can fail and try again. The rule of law and cultural norms protect the freedom to compete. And this dynamic generates relentless reinvention.

I have personally worked with founders and CEOs of over 50 Chinese companies. Quietly, many of them ask the same question: *"Should I send my wife or my son first?"* What they mean is, how can their families begin a life in America. That tells you everything. They see something here they can't get at home. The freedom to dream, act, and succeed beyond their imagination.

America is the world's largest melting pot. The only nation where a Chinese immigrant becomes American, where an Indian becomes American, where cognitive diversity from every corner of the globe fuses into something entirely new. America formalizes risk-taking.

Venture capital, legal protections, transparent failure and bankruptcy rules—these are tools that allow reinvention. This **multiethnic, multicognitive environment** powers creativity at scale. Immigrants see this and flood in. According to the American Immigration Council, nearly 45 percent of Fortune 500 companies were founded by immigrants or their children.[119]

In contrast, China is closing its doors. In early 2025, the CCP restricted international travel for top AI researchers. Even the founder of DeepSeek declined an invitation to attend an AI summit in Paris. The CCP fears influence and leakage. This fear is its weakness.

China recruits foreign talent, but they remain temporary, linked to narrow technology areas, and always under surveillance. Russia couldn't build this. Japan couldn't build this. The **mono-ethnic, mono-cultural societies do not have this advantage**. Even Europe and the UK, diverse as they are, cannot match America's fusion.

Ultimately, this is a **contest between two models**. One open, self-renewing, and distributed. The other top-down, autocratic, and closed. In the long run, openness will win. Because innovation is not born from fear.

5. America's Administrative and Governance System

I have worked across dozens of countries and industries. The one constant I hear from foreign leaders and businesspeople is this: The US legal system is the most trusted in the world. And they are right.

Yes, it has flaws. It's divided between central and federal powers. Fifty states, each with its own rules. Could America be more efficient with a dictatorship? Sure. For about five years. Then it would collapse under its own rigidity and lack of correction. But its independence, transparency, and accessibility are unmatched. Anyone, citizen or foreigner, can go all the way to the Supreme Court. And many do. That is why people want to invest in the US. That is why talent wants to stay.

The system renews itself. Administrations change. Policies shift. But the machinery of governance—regulators, public institutions, civil servants—keeps running. New leaders bring fresh eyes. The system tests itself constantly. Better ideas surface. The country learns.

This messy, self-correcting rhythm is a strength. It slows decisions, yes. But it builds durability. America's foundational principle is transparency. Investigative journalism, public trials, legal checks—they force accountability.

Look at the Watergate investigation. It led to the resignation of a president. In how many countries is that possible through a legal and journalistic process? This is, in the parlance of competitive analysis, a **core strength**.

Even now, with stronger executive action underway to confront China's rise, the democratic process remains intact. Midterm elections will be held in November 2026. The next presidential election in 2028. Leadership may change. But the governance system will continue to evolve. It's built for that.

China does not believe this. The CCP is betting that America will fracture. That leadership changes will undo progress. But this is a misread. Despite the division, despite the messiness, this system wins. What looks like churn is actually strength. Because it keeps the system adaptive and self-healing.

6. The Power of Trusted Alliances

Together with its allies, America commands the largest market, deepest technology base, and most sophisticated consumers in the world. This sphere of aligned democracies already far exceeds China in economic and technological power. It is home to the most productive companies, most trusted institutions, and most sought-after markets. And critically, it is where future demand will come from.

What matters is intent. And as of fall 2025, Washington has been expanding trade agreements with key partners while pressing others, like India, in tough negotiations. The tariff regime under President Trump has created strains with some allies. But one strategic intent behind this approach is clear: to force allies out of complacency enabled by currency advantages and decades of America subsidizing their defense.

These are not signs of erosion. They are **recalibrations**. Toward fairness. Toward resilience. Toward stronger allies with stronger currencies who carry their own weight.

America needs allies not just for defense, but for balanced trade, supply-chain resilience, and joint innovation. And these allies know it. The US and Europe rallied quickly in the face of Russian aggression. It was driven by shared values and shared threats. Despite current tensions between America and India, that relationship will strengthen. Trump and Modi have stated their goal of $500 billion in bilateral trade with India by 2030.

Consider semiconductors. China cannot build an end to end chip capability without Taiwan's TSMC, the Netherlands' ASML, and US-based Applied Materials. This trio represents generations of IP, tools, and scientific insight. It's a roadblock China cannot bypass.

If Washington, the Dutch, and the Taiwanese decided tomorrow to fully cut off advanced tech access to China, the CCP's progress would stall for decades. The alliance has that power.

Already, we see reshoring. The CHIPS Act ($52 billion in incentives), TSMC's $100 billion commitment to build five new plants, and Nvidia's $500 billion AI server push in the US are proof. Supply chains are shifting, fast.

The **collective strength** of America and its allies can block China's path, not through containment, but through competition on terms America sets.

WHY THESE STRENGTHS HAVEN'T BEEN USED

The answer lies not in America's lack of strength, but in its failure to deploy it. Power unused is power wasted. And four forces have kept America paralyzed.

First, a lack of courageous leadership across three phases. For two decades, American leadership failed in succession. Initially, **naivety**, believing China would play by the rules once integrated into global trade. Then came the strategic objective of bringing China into democracy through economic engagement, the idea that prosperity would liberalize the regime. Finally, even when the threat was highlighted, as early as 2015, America failed to see China's coordinated moves under the radar. Leadership recognized the threat but lacked the courage to act decisively until Trump's administration began pushing back.

The Biden administration followed many of Trump's policies affecting China, but remained incremental, always constrained by **fear** that aggressive action could trigger a third world war. The reality is this: Confronting China may require going to the brink. No one knows how far it will go. But **paralysis guarantees defeat**.

I have sat in rooms with respected CEOs and board members and sensed a quiet awe of China's momentum and creeping resignation that the US can't catch up. They say things like, *"Maybe we just need to accept that China will lead and find a way to coexist."* That is defeatism. And it is dangerous.

Second, sluggish and fragmented policy. America has taken steps—the CHIPS Act, the Inflation Reduction Act, and others—but the actions are reactive, fragmented, and slow. Legislation exists. Bipartisan support is growing. But without consistent, focused execution from the executive branch and state-level agencies, the impact is diluted.

The Huawei saga is emblematic. The US warned its allies in 2019, but the rollout of bans and removals dragged on for years. Germany only recently committed to phasing out Huawei equipment by 2029. Policy needs to do more than signal intent. It must close the gaps.

Third, institutional blindness. For too long, institutions across government, media, and business refused to see this for what it is: a coordinated, long-term economic assault. Many still don't. Some cling to the illusion that the Chinese market will bounce back, or that Beijing can be coaxed into playing fair.

In 2024, Congress exposed that over $3 billion from American VC firms had gone into Chinese firms tied to military and surveillance. Nearly $2 billion went into AI startups with direct PLA applications.[120] What part of this still looks like a misunderstanding?

Fourth, the grip of shareholder value. CEOs are judged by quarterly earnings and stock prices. The incentive structures are built around maximizing valuation, not national resilience. CEOs may personally see the threat from China, but unless policy forces action, they cannot act. Because if they do, and revenues fall, they will be punished by the market. The shareholder value doctrine overrides patriotism.

Take Nvidia. After the US banned exports of advanced chips, Nvidia created a lower-powered H800 chip to sidestep restrictions. In May 2025, Nvidia announced plans to open a research center in Shanghai, even as Chinese authorities launched an antitrust investigation against it. Why would Nvidia do this? Because the grip of shareholder value is stronger than the risk of national security exposure.

THE TURNING POINT

When you see these four forces—timid leadership, weak policy, institutional blindness, and shareholder supremacy—you realize why America is lagging. Not because of its adversary's superiority, but because of its own **inaction**.

There is a line often attributed to Winston Churchill: *America will always do the right thing, after exhausting all other possibilities.* That has been the pattern here. Every option has been tried except the one that goes directly after the core of China's power—its 90 Percent Model.

Let me be clear: China's strategy has been working. The 90 Percent Model has gutted industries, the encirclement is real, and the psychological warfare has planted doubt in boardrooms across the West. But the eclipse of America's power is not inevitable. The arsenal exists. The strengths I have just outlined are real, renewable, and if properly deployed, overwhelming. What has been missing is not capability. It is will.

As entrepreneur and venture capitalist Marc Andreessen put it in the *Lex Fridman* podcast, *"We went from a country that believed it could do anything to a country that believes it can't do anything."*

And yet, change is beginning. The signs are faint but real. Some managements are waking up. Some funds are reallocating. Media coverage is gradually sharpening. Economic analysts are raising red flags. The broader public, which for a long time was not directly affected, is now beginning to sense the threat. The pain is starting to reach households.

The strengths of America are unbounded. What has been lacking is **leadership and courage**. Now the question is: Will the country follow through?

In the next chapter, we will see that the tide is indeed turning. Not just in Washington, but in boardrooms, in state capitals, and among America's allies. The arsenal is being activated. The question is whether it will be deployed with the speed and force this moment demands.

Chapter 9

The Tide Is Turning

America has the arsenal. You have seen it. Market access, global financial control, capital discipline, open institutions, melting pot culture, trusted governance, and battle-tested alliances. These are real weapons, sitting ready to be deployed.

For two decades, they sat unused. Leadership hesitated. Policy drifted. Institutions looked the other way. And the shareholder value rise kept CEOs frozen in place, unwilling to act even when the threat was clear.

But something has shifted. The tide is turning. Not everywhere. Not all at once. But the **signs are unmistakable**. In Washington, in boardrooms, among allies, and even in the factories and supply chains where the economic war is being fought on the ground. The response is beginning.

This chapter is about that shift. What is driving it. What is working. What remains fragile. And why, even with this momentum, America cannot win alone.

THE DISRUPTOR IN THE WHITE HOUSE

Donald Trump broke the pattern. In his first term, he sounded the alarm. In his second, he has moved faster than any president since Reagan, deploying state power with startling speed. By virtue of his election alone, the world braced. He had said it again and again: Tariffs would be his primary weapon. The first 90 days confirmed it.

The coherence is not immediately understood because the tariff back-and-forth causes confusion. But there is method in what appears to be madness. I suggest the reader master this: What lies beneath Trump's approach is a systematic strategy to force currency parity and end decades of manipulated trade.

February and March 2025: two rounds of blanket tariffs on Chinese imports, 10 percent each, to jolt Beijing off balance. April: escalation to an average of 145 percent when China shrugged off the signal. May brought a truce in Geneva—tariffs stepped back to 30 percent on the US side, 10 percent on China's, and talks began. By June, a new baseline emerged: US at 55 percent, China at 10 percent, with negotiations widening into currency, critical minerals, and excess-capacity dumping.

The numbers may change, but the pattern is clear: **shock, negotiate, recalibrate, repeat**. Tariffs are not the end state. They are the crowbar that forces Beijing to the table. And once there, the real negotiations begin—over tech restrictions, critical minerals, and the supply-chain choke points that matter most.

Critics ask: Why this apparent chaos? Why such punishing tariffs? The answer requires understanding what was covered in Part I: The **WTO has miserably failed.** Its rules-based order has been destroyed. International trade has been manipulated for decades through currency disparity, subsidies, and dumping.

Without currency parity, no trade deal can last. Almost every major trading partner—China, Japan, Taiwan, Europe—has used currency disparity against the dollar to sustain surpluses. Other tools exist—WTO disputes, currency interventions—but none have an immediate enforcement mechanism. Tariffs are the enforcement tool. They close the gap country by country, deal by deal, and force reciprocity (see Exhibit 24: tariff by country[121]).

Exhibit 24: US Tariff Rate by Select Countries, August 2025

US Import Partners by Trade Volume and Tariff Rates
Share of Total US Imports and Applied Tariff Rates by Country

Country/Region	Share of US Imports		Tariff Rate
■ Mexico	15.5%	▬	25%
■ China	13.4%	▬	30%
■ Canada	12.6%	▲	35%
Germany	4.9%	▼	15%
Japan	4.5%	▼	15%
Vietnam	4.2%	▬	20%
South Korea	4.0%	▼	15%
Taiwan	3.6%	▬	20%
Ireland	3.2%	▼	15%
India	2.7%	▲	50%
Italy	2.3%	▼	15%
United Kingdom	2.1%	▼	10%
Switzerland	1.9%	▲	39%
Thailand	1.9%	▬	19%
France	1.8%	▼	15%
Malaysia	1.6%	▬	19%
Singapore	1.3%	▼	10%
Brazil	1.3%	▲	50%
Netherland	1.0%	▼	15%
Other Countries	<1% each	▼	10–40%

Visual Guide

■ Top 3 Import Partners ▼ Low Tariffs (10–15%) ▲ High Tariffs (31%+)
■ China (Strategic Focus) ▬ Medium Tariffs (16–30%)

Source: BBC Visual Journalism

Trump's logic is **specific, measurable, and verifiable**. Exporting countries must bring currencies into line with the dollar. Tariffs remain until parity is achieved. In parallel, secure foreign investment into the US, boosting American growth while giving partners market access. As currencies strengthen, partners move up the value chain, exporting higher-value goods without subsidies or manipulation. Trade balances narrow toward zero. When that happens, tariffs go away.

There is another structural flaw worth examining. Today's tariffs are paid by American importers, not Chinese exporters. This could be reversed—call it a duty on imports, collected at the point of export. There is no law preventing this; it is man-made tradition. Reversing it would make Chinese exports pay the cost, not American buyers, directly attacking the 90 Percent Model at its source.

It is the first time in decades that the US has applied pressure at the exact point of leverage: the global currency gap and the trade imbalances it sustains.

Most people link the lower prices of Chinese imports to subsidies and internal destructive competition. They miss the point. Unless **currency parity alignment** is achieved with China, Taiwan, Japan, Europe, and others, there will be no trade surplus correction.

Singapore shows what happens when parity is embraced. From the 1970s onward, its dollar appreciated from roughly 3 to 1.35 against the US dollar. The stronger currency allowed Singapore to buy better technology, move up the value chain, and compete in first-world markets. Taiwan and South Korea followed similar paths, transforming into high-value exporters. What seemed a penalty at first became the foundation of prosperity.

Trump is betting that others will follow that arc, forced at first by tariffs, then rewarded as their economies mature.

SIX PRIORITIES THAT DRIVE THE MACHINE

Behind the tariff headlines sits a broader plan. I have discerned five interconnected priorities at the heart of Trump's approach. It is not perfect. But it is coherent. It is coordinated. And it is forcing both allies and adversaries to respond.

First, fixing the fundamentals. Trump is working to rebuild America's financial foundation. As of late 2025, he has repeatedly urged the Federal Reserve to lower interest rates, arguing that high borrowing costs are inflating the federal debt-servicing burden, while the Fed resists, citing its mandate to control inflation and maintain independence. He argues that his pressure has prevented the deficit from growing even larger, though independent estimates do not clearly quantify the difference such actions have made. The actual federal deficit may not have been cut, but without these actions, it could have been significantly worse.

Meanwhile, Trump is making America a more attractive place to invest. Tariff revenues tripled between March and June 2025, reaching nearly $27 billion in June alone (see Exhibit 25: tariff revenue surge[122]). At that run rate, the annual pace is above $300 billion, roughly four times last year's. His "big, beautiful bill"—a set of tax cuts expected to save US businesses around $100 billion this year—makes it easier for firms to carry more of the tariff burden rather than pass it on to consumers.

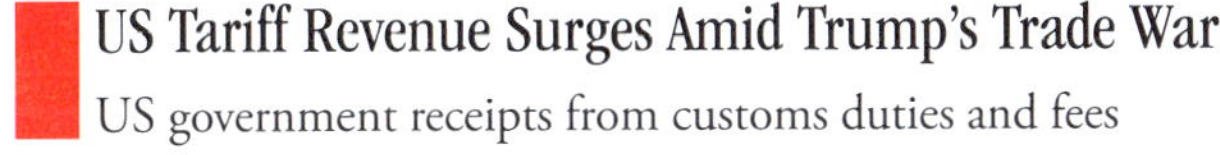

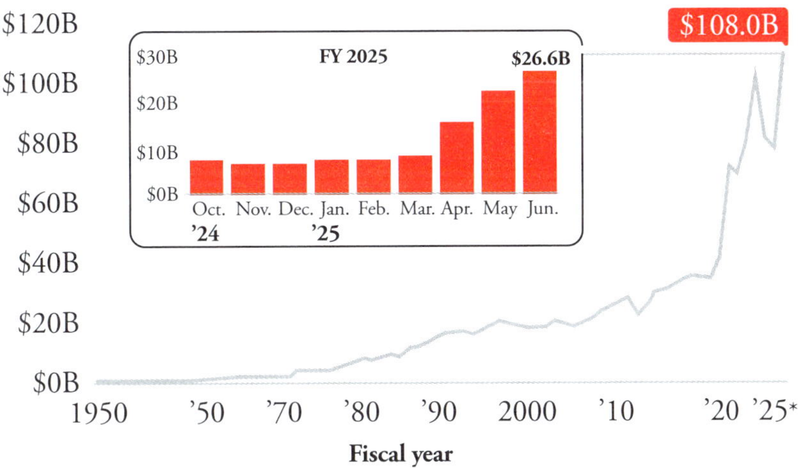

* Data for FY2025 data through June 30. Fiscal year ends September 30.
Source: US Department of the Treasury

Second, rebuilding America's economic growth and industrialization. And the vehicle is investment. Trump is driving a historic surge of capital, domestic and foreign, into US operations. Investment brings technology, know-how, talent, and the manufacturing base America needs to compete.

The Commerce Department's Investment Accelerator Unit is fast-tracking projects over $1 billion, eliminating regulatory delays at federal and state levels. What once took years now takes months.

As of late 2025, nearly **$9 trillion in new investments**, domestic and foreign, have been announced (see Exhibit 26: investment surge[123]). Nvidia, SoftBank and OpenAI's Stargate Project, Apple, players from the UAE, Qatar, and Japan—all pouring capital into US operations. Japan's July 2025 commitment of $550 billion, structured as a sovereign investment fund deployable at the discretion of the US president, is solving what once seemed unsolvable: the funding bottleneck.

Exhibit 26: Major Investment Announcements in Trump's Second Term

Select Investments

Name	Investment	Focus
UAE	$1.4 Trillion	Technology, aerospace, energy
Japan	$1 Trillion	Auto plants, US steel
Apple	$600 Billion	Manufacturing
Meta	$600 Billion	AI infrastructure, workforce expansion
Saudi Arabia	$600 Billion	Technology, manufacturing
SoftBank/OpenAI/Oracle	$500 Billion	AI infrastructure (Stargate)

Nvidia	$500 Billion	AI, supercomputers
Micron	$200 Billion	Semiconductor manufacturing

Source: The White House

Third, energy is the foundation of economic leverage and growth. Trump recognized early that no country achieves economic growth without abundant, affordable energy. He revived a strategic truth: Fossil fuels will remain America's main engine for growth. He reversed years of declining investment in fossil fuel production by opening new areas for exploration, streamlining permitting processes, and removing regulatory barriers that had choked domestic energy expansion.

The Environmental Protection Agency has been sidelined. Climate targets dialed down. Trump opened the Gulf of Mexico, rebranded as the *"Gulf of America,"* for aggressive production. He accelerated approvals for drilling in Alaska and the Arctic National Wildlife Reserve. He greenlit new pipelines. He removed restrictions that had made American liquefied natural gas (LNG) exports slower and more expensive than competitors'.

He also streamlined energy flows from Russia and other suppliers to Europe, reducing Europe's energy crisis while maintaining pressure on Moscow. The strategy is multilayered: Abundant American energy weakens OPEC's pricing power, reduces Europe's dependence on adversaries, and funds America's reindustrialization. Cheap, reliable energy attracts manufacturing back to US soil.

Trump is using energy to shift global geopolitics. His wager: Saudi Arabia, for defense and technology access, will tilt back toward Washington. Stable American energy production will undercut Russia's leverage over Europe while tariffs pressure India to stop buying Russian crude. Low energy prices will keep American industry competitive while China struggles with higher input costs.

As Marc Andreessen noted, *"We can be energy independent anytime we want . . . It's purely a question of choice."* And Trump has made that choice.

Fourth, breaking China's choke hold on strategic resources. Trump understands that China's dominance in rare earths and critical minerals is the single most dangerous choke hold America faces. These materials are the lifeblood of military systems, semiconductor manufacturing, renewable energy, and advanced technology. Without them, America cannot build weapons, chips, or electric vehicles. China controls the supply. That must end.

His answer: Move fast to secure alternative supplies from Canada, Greenland, and Latin America. Build processing facilities at home to eliminate dependence on Chinese refining. We detail the path forward to breaking the choke holds in Part III of the book.

Fifth, rebuilding military strength. Defense investment is ramping up. Trump has pushed NATO members to spend 5 percent of GDP on defense—up from the previous 2 percent target (see

Exhibit 27: NATO Defense Underspending[124]). At home, he has proposed a 13 percent increase in US defense spending for FY2026, pushing the Pentagon budget past $1 trillion for the first time.[125]

Exhibit 27: NATO Defense Underspending

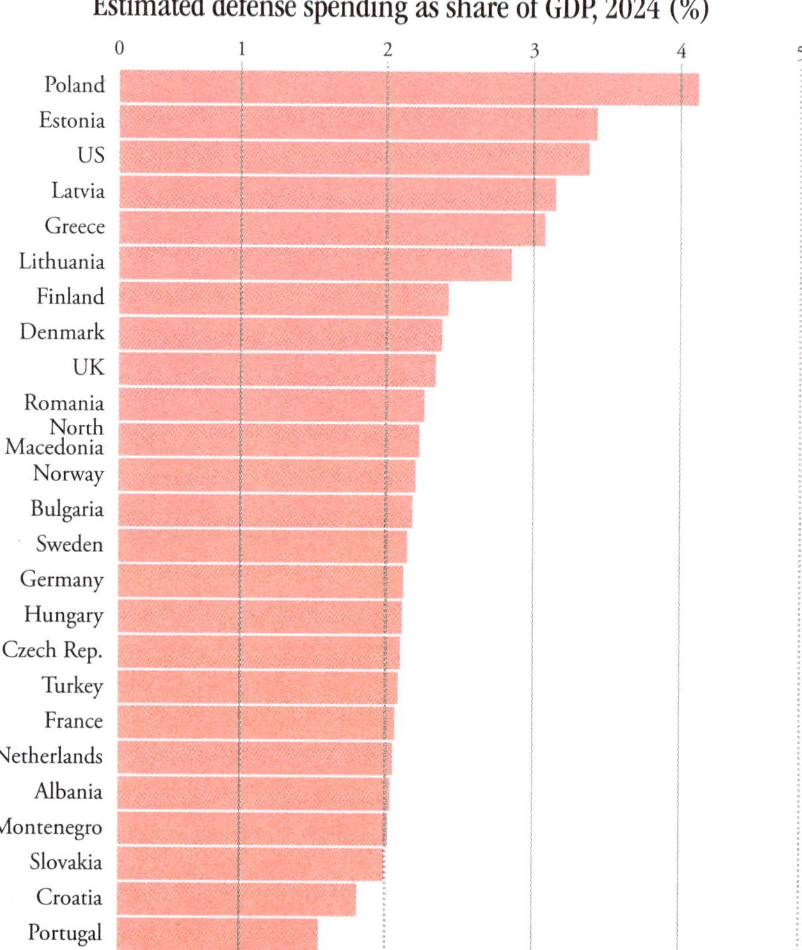

Source: *Financial Times*, "Trump Wants 5% NATO Defence Spending Target, Europe Told"

Sixth, closing technology conscription. The final priority is shutting down the transfer of US technology to China. This goes far beyond chips. Trump is pushing to identify and restrict every technology with dual-use potential—AI, quantum, data architectures, semiconductors. Controls must be deep, specific, and enforced. Product by product. Relationship by relationship. National security overrides quarterly earnings.

EARLY SIGNALS OF SHIFT

The immediate effects are already visible. With the RMB under pressure, the People's Bank of China is pressuring state banks to buy yuan, sending daily warning signals to traders, and quietly guiding the rate. Meanwhile, key partners such as Taiwan show early signs of currency appreciation—roughly 8 percent.

In July 2025, the US-China Business Council's annual survey found that only 48 percent of US companies plan to invest in China this year, a sharp drop from 80 percent in 2024 and the lowest level recorded since the survey began.[126] Multinationals are moving capital.

Allies are recalibrating. In April 2025, South Korea and Vietnam launched parallel crackdowns on transshipments aimed at circumventing US tariffs on China. Seoul created a dedicated customs task force, while Hanoi issued new directives to tighten origin checks and avoid anti-dumping penalties. Moves like these were unthinkable just a year earlier.

THE SYSTEM IS ADJUSTING

But Trump is not the whole story. The American system itself is beginning to adjust. Congress, despite its divisions, has moved with surprising speed on China-related legislation. The CHIPS Act, the Inflation Reduction Act, export controls on advanced semiconductors—these are bipartisan moves that are rare in today's Washington.

State governments are stepping up. Governors are negotiating directly with foreign investors, offering incentives for domestic manufacturing, and building supply-chain resilience at the local level. Michigan, Ohio, Pennsylvania, Wisconsin—these states are becoming the hotbeds for industrial renewal.

The Small Business Administration's Made in America Manufacturing Initiative, launched in March 2025, aims to ease $100 billion worth of regulatory burdens, improve access to capital through loan programs, and establish a new Office of Manufacturing and Trade. A digital portal now connects firms with over a million domestic suppliers. This is policy backed by execution.

Advanced "lights-out" manufacturers like Protolabs (specifics in Chapter 12) have quietly built the infrastructure and digital capability to manufacture at home. Fast, precise, and at scale. What's needed now is policy protection and focused capital. The rest—talent, technology, and speed—America already has.

BUSINESSES ARE SHIFTING STANCE

And it's not just policy. Businesses are changing tactics. Some by choice. Others by force. But the pattern is **unmistakable**.

The wave of corporate exits from China is real and accelerating. Daimler Truck announced in July 2025 that it is actively considering a full manufacturing exit. Mitsubishi Motors fully exited China the same month by terminating its engine joint venture. Mercedes-Benz is cutting 10–15 percent of sales and finance jobs in China. Nippon Steel ended its half-century joint venture with Baoshan Iron & Steel. IBM closed its 1,000-person China R&D center. Microsoft, Dell, Stanley Black & Decker, Airbnb—all have undertaken significant pullbacks.

Hewlett-Packard is moving decisively. By the end of fiscal 2025, 90 percent of its production for North America will be outside China. Only one-tenth will originate from China as HP builds a diversified supply chain to reduce geopolitical exposure.

The American Chamber of Commerce in China reports that 30 percent of US companies have initiated or are planning relocation of manufacturing and sourcing in 2024–2025.[127] The primary destinations include Southeast Asia, India, and the US itself.

We will examine these stories in detail in Chapter 11. For now, understand this: These are not isolated incidents. This is a trend. And it is being driven not just by policy pressure, but by a **fundamental reassessment of risk**.

Some CEOs are acting early, protecting their core assets and finding new growth paths. Others are being forced out by blacklists, regulatory harassment, or rule changes. Regardless of the trigger, the result is the same. **The great unwinding** has begun.

MY TAKE: WHAT'S WORKING, WHAT'S FRAGILE

As a student of strategy and execution, I focus on the one thing that cuts through the noise: the actions of the leader. What are they doing? What are they actually trying to achieve? What methods do they keep coming back to? Strip away the chatter, the headlines, the partisanship. Look at the actions. Then deduce the method.

President Trump's approach to China represents the most decisive strategic shift by any US administration in decades. And while the results are still unfolding, his intent is unmistakable. He is doing what no president before him dared: confronting China's 90 percent overcapacity model with speed, force, and focus.

What's Working

With President Trump, the **objective is crystal clear**. He has said it again and again. He wants to stop China's dumping of excess production into global markets. He knows that dumping hollows out US industries, corrodes American jobs, and deepens the trade imbalance that funds China's rise. His goal is to shrink that imbalance and push China to compete on new terms.

And how is he doing it? By matching China's tactics, industry by industry, flow by flow. Tariffs on direct exports. Sanctions on transshipments through proxies. Relentless pressure. The message is simple: If you flood our markets, we will retaliate.

It is not a one-size-fits-all foreign policy about import reduction. It is a laser-sharp attack. Item by item. Proxy country by proxy country. Industry by industry.

According to *Bloomberg Economics*, if Trump succeeds in targeting these transshipments with tighter controls and higher levies, it could threaten 70 percent of China's exports to the US and shave off over 2.1 percent of its GDP.

In July 2025, the administration announced a 40 percent tariff on Chinese goods transshipped via third countries to evade duties. It's a direct assault on the China-plus-one strategy, where Chinese exporters use offshore factories predominantly in Southeast Asia and Latin America to dodge US tariffs.

This is new. Earlier administrations used broad language—"managing China's rise," "strategic competition," "decoupling," "de-risking." They convened dialogues, issued vague communiqués, and worried more about global consensus than targeted action. And the result? A trillion-dollar trade surplus for China, the hollowing out of US industry, and a steady psychological erosion of American confidence.

Trump is not doing that. He is not negotiating from a podium. He is applying force. Economic, political, and, when needed, military.

Much of Washington's foreign policy elite struggles to understand Trump's approach. These experts are shaped by legacy institutions, not by supply chains or manufacturing floors. They look for doctrine. A blueprint. A white paper. And they default to caution and consensus.

But Trump is doing none of that. There is no grand strategy document. There are no sweeping speeches to the UN. What there is, is movement. Relentless pressure. Actions taken. The tactics vary, the goals don't.

That confuses people. In their mind, Trump is inconsistent. Incoherent. Too transactional. But they're missing the point. He will do whatever it takes to reduce the Chinese trade surplus, slow down industrial dumping, and get allies to rebalance. That is the goal. Whether the method is tariffs, tech bans, rerouted supply chains, or back-channel threats, the goal stays the same.

Most presidents lead through themes. They announce a worldview, convene allies, and aim to build consensus. Trump is taking the fight directly to the point of pressure. If China reroutes exports through Vietnam, the pressure moves there. If companies cluster around a loophole, the next tariff hits that cluster. It's targeted, kinetic, and fast.

What's Fragile

But here is the hard truth. Right now, **China has the upper hand** in negotiations. They control the world's flow of critical raw materials. They can shut off magnets, solar inputs, battery precursors, and immediately stall industries in the West. And America is not prepared for it.

When Trump raised tariffs to 145 percent, China retaliated strategically. They cut off key materials. They slowed exports to US allies. They showed they can halt an industry without firing a shot. Trump, in response, was **forced to adjust**—on visas, on oil from Iran, even on sensitive technologies. The game is not one-sided.

Trump has acknowledged this reality. He admitted he had been "lying in the weeds," believing engagement would work while China exploited American openness. He was **naive**. He was taken for a ride.

Don't mistake that for Trump being cornered. He has shown, repeatedly, that he is willing to go to the edge. He has weapons: financial, diplomatic, and military. And just as China controls materials that can stall Western industries, America and its allies control inputs that can halt China's manufacturing machine. We detail these **reverse choke points** in Part III. America still holds superiority across these arenas. And if China does not change its behavior, I believe Trump will move to those options.

But the **deeper issue** is this: Is Trump building the long-term strength America needs? That's where the jury is still out. The real game is industrial revival. And here, America's pace is still **sluggish**.

There is no national blueprint. No sweeping initiative to out-build China in critical industries. Without that, tariffs are a delay tactic, not a solution. The 90 Percent Model may be slowed, but it won't be dismantled unless the US and its allies build and rebuild at scale.

What's Missing

Trump's approach has another **critical gap**: He has not taken the public with him. Most Americans still don't understand the core problem. They see tariffs and think inflation. They see headlines about trade wars and assume it's political theater. But few grasp what is really at stake.

At the heart of the problem with China and its allies is currency manipulation and disparity. Unless that is controlled, the trade deficit will not reduce, and America will continue to be hollowed out. Trump's approach is tariffs. But without **public buy-in**, without clarity on the problem itself, the political will to sustain this pressure could evaporate.

He needs to explain it. Repeatedly. Clearly. In terms that every voter, every CEO, every journalist can understand. This is not about trade policy. It is about survival.

Allied alignment is also essential. Not only for economic diversification but also for counterbalancing China across regions. Yet Trump's latest tariff moves, like the 50 percent duties levied on Indian exports in August 2025, have rattled key partners. Pressure tactics may win short-term leverage, but if they **alienate** those whose support is vital, the strategy weakens from within.

This is the **contradiction at the heart of his method**: urgency and precision on one side, unpredictability that undercuts trust on the other. The alignment premise still holds, but execution becomes harder, and outcomes less certain.

THE LEADERSHIP QUESTION

Trump is forcing action. But he cannot do this alone. And this is where business leaders must step up.

You are on the front line of this economic war. Every decision you make—where to invest, where to source, which markets to prioritize—affects the outcome. You have contributed to China's rise, often unknowingly, sometimes knowingly. Now you can help stall its march.

The bind you face is real. I understand that. Staying in China means losing control. Leaving means taking a hit. But the cost of inaction is worse. Because the longer you wait, the more leverage you lose.

Some CEOs are acting. They are extricating from China, finding new growth markets, and protecting their core assets. Others are still frozen, hoping the storm will pass. It won't. The dilemma will only deepen.

This is not just Trump's fight. It is yours. Your board's. Your investors'. And it requires the same level of courage and clarity that Trump is bringing to the policy arena.

WHY CONVERGENCE IS NECESSARY

No matter how long it takes, and whatever it costs—inflation, higher prices, short-term pain—the US and its allies **must break the 90 Percent Model**. There is no alternative. I believe it can be broken. The talent exists. The capital exists. The world's best innovators are still knocking on America's door, including those from China itself.

But Trump's approach alone is insufficient. China has demonstrated it can block any industry at will. The choke hold on magnets is just one example. There will be more. And unless America builds resilience across the board, unless it coordinates with allies to rebuild industrial capacity at scale, the pressure will not hold.

That is what the next chapter is about. Not Trump's strategy, but the broader coalition strategy that must now take shape. Because without it, even the most aggressive tariffs, the most decisive leadership, and the most committed businesses will not be enough.

The tide is turning. But turning is not winning. **To win, America must lead a convergence unlike any the world has seen since World War II.** And that convergence must begin now.

Chapter 10

No Convergence, No Future

Trump has forced the issue. Businesses are shifting. Allies are recalibrating. The American system is adjusting. But momentum alone does not guarantee success. Trump's approach is bold, targeted, and creates pressure. But it has a fatal flaw: **America is fighting alone**.

Tariffs can slow China's march. They cannot stop it. Financial sanctions can hurt Beijing. They cannot break the 90 Percent Excess Production Capacity Model. Even the most aggressive unilateral action will hit limits—because China holds choke points across multiple industries, and no single country has the scale to rebuild what has been lost.

This is not a contest between two countries. It is a contest between two systems: market-based democracies and Xi's communist command economy. And the outcome will not be decided by one leader, one policy, or one nation. It will be decided by convergence.

Industrial convergence. Military convergence. Technological convergence. Control of global logistics, financial flows, and information infrastructure. The alignment of the free world's economic power, built on trust, coordinated across borders, and executed with the urgency this moment demands.

That is what this chapter is about.

TWO SPHERES ARE EMERGING

The world is hardening into two spheres: economically, militarily, and ideologically. The space for neutrality is shrinking fast.

One sphere is democratically led, anchored by the US, representing roughly **$60 trillion in GDP**. The other is led by communist China, pulling together an axis including Russia, Venezuela, Iran, and North Korea, with about **$25 trillion in GDP**. Between them lie another 180 countries with **$25 trillion in combined GDP**. Many of these will choose sides based on convenience and short-term interest, coerced by Xi or attracted by Trump. But the choice is coming.

The **American Sphere** is a center of gravity. At its core are six economic powers: **the United States, the European Union, Japan, South Korea, Israel, and the United Kingdom**.

Together, this bloc commands capital, technology, rule of law, and defense partnerships that China cannot match. They are home to the most productive companies, most trusted institutions, and most sought-after markets. And critically, they are where future demand will come from.

This framing is not scientific or rigid. It is directional. Others—Taiwan, India, Singapore, Indonesia—may not be listed here as core members, but they form part of the ecosystem. Rare earth producing countries like Australia, Canada, and those in Latin America will also align, driven by China's monopolistic behavior and coercive trade practices. Many will tilt toward the American Sphere in trade and values. What matters is not the exact list, but the alignment it represents.

But here is what matters most: **Together, this bloc has the resources to counter China**. Separately, they do not.

WHAT CONVERGENCE IS

Convergence is not an abstract call for unity. It is the only meaningful counterweight to China's 90 Percent Model and industrial choke hold. This fight will not be won by general declarations or vague commitments. It must be waged through **coordinated, industry-specific, multilateral action**.

Convergence means coordinated economic planning across governments, corporations, and allied nations. It is a practical playbook for:

- Building **fast, networked, and competitive** industrial capacity designed to displace China's choke points through coordinated manufacturing and joint investment in the very sectors where China seeks dominance.

- **Aligning tariff regimes** to block subsidized dumping.
- **Filtering investments** to protect sensitive technologies.
- **Setting shared technology standards**, so Beijing does not write the rules of the future.
- **Mapping collective exposure** to Chinese supply chains and designing exits. Not from all trade with China, but from critical dependencies that can be weaponized.

Convergence is not isolationism. It is **selective self-sufficiency at scale**. Only convergence delivers the speed, credibility, and scale required to break China's momentum.

Think of it this way: What NATO and AUKUS have done for military coordination, convergence must do for industrial coordination. The alliances already exist. The defense infrastructure is in place. Now it must extend into the trade and industrial arena.

Trump has embraced parts of this vision. High tariffs forced China into unsustainable inventories. The 2025 tariff truce, though temporary, gave the US breathing room. But the 90 Percent Model will not collapse voluntarily. It must be dismantled through **collective action**.

CHAPTER 10

WHY CONVERGENCE IS NEEDED

President Xi is banking that convergence will not happen. He believes that America will fracture its alliances. That Europe will hedge. That Japan and South Korea will prioritize their own trade balances over collective security. That the UK will pursue its own path. That differences will outweigh common interests.

And so far, he has been partly right. Trump's tariff moves on allies—50 percent duties on India, pressure on Europe, friction with South Korea—have created tension. The very partners America needs most have been rattled by unpredictability.

But Xi's bet also reveals his weakness. He knows that if the American Sphere comes together, if these six economic powerhouses coordinate their policies and align their industrial strategies, China's model breaks. The 90 percent overcapacity machine loses its markets. The choke hold on critical materials loses its leverage. The psychological warfare loses its punch.

This is a long haul. A **tit-for-tat fight** that will stretch for years, even decades (see Exhibit 28: Tariff and Non-Tariff Tit-for-Tat[128]). Each side will keep pressing where it hurts most, negotiating over items that can throttle the opponent's economy. To sustain such a war, both will rely on the machinery that underpins power itself: **industrial capacity, agriculture, energy, and water security**. These are instruments of endurance.

In September 2025, the Netherlands invoked a Cold War–era emergency law to seize control of Nexperia, a Chinese-owned chipmaker critical to Europe's auto industry. Beijing retaliated immediately, blocking chip exports from Nexperia's Chinese facilities. European automakers faced production halts. Within weeks, both sides eased restrictions and agreed to talks. The pattern repeats: **action, retaliation, negotiation**. Neither side can afford a full rupture, yet neither will back down. This is the tit-for-tat that defines the contest.

Exhibit 28: Tariff & Non-Tariff Tit-for-Tat

*All or most imports (excluding those with separate tariffs, granted exceptions)
Source: The Tax Foundation, CNN

Non-Tariff Tit-for-Tat: Action, Reaction, Action

Domain	US Strike	China's Counter
Tech & Chips	Blocked exports to 140+ Chinese firms, restricting critical technology	Launched antitrust probe into US chipmakers; added firms to blacklists
Export Controls	Blacklisted Chinese firms; tightened global tech access	Added US firms to China's "Unreliable Entity List"; restricted licenses
Critical Minerals	Declared dependency on critical minerals a national security threat	Banned exports of gallium, germanium, graphite, and other battery/rare earth materials
EVs & Clean Tech	Proposed tariffs on electric vehicles and solar panels	Cut off or restricted exports of battery materials and related clean tech components
Agriculture Trade	Raised tariffs on agricultural imports; promoted reshoring of production	Shifted soy, corn, and other agricultural purchases to Brazil, Argentina, and others
Digital & Data	Enforced bans (e.g., TikTok) and data restrictions on Chinese apps/companies	Tightened foreign data laws; censored or restricted US firms' operations in China
Finance & Capital	Blocked US pension funds from investing in China; investment restrictions	Raised capital barriers; intensified auditing and regulatory crackdowns on foreign investors

Source: Author's analysis

The danger is real. The ultimate risk is escalation. Financial sanctions that cut off China's liquidity. Retaliation that shuts down Western industries. And if that fails to produce a resolution, the risk of military conflict rises. The clouds of war are not hypothetical. Taiwan, the Philippines, Japan, Russia-Ukraine—these are not separate stories. They are all China-driven. The chessboard is moving.

Let me be clear: The Ukraine war is not just Russia's war. It is China's war, fought through a proxy. Beijing funds it, enables it, and uses it to distract and drain the West. Every dollar, every missile, every sanction package diverted to Ukraine is one less focused on China.

This is why **convergence is not optional**. America cannot prevent China's advance alone. No single country can sustain this level of economic and geopolitical pressure. But together, the six-power bloc can.

WHERE CONVERGENCE MUST FOCUS

Convergence must focus on the industries where China holds choke-hold power and where the free world must rebuild capacity.

This includes the 10 industries China has explicitly targeted in its *Made in China 2025* plan—EVs, renewables, biopharma, aerospace, AI, robotics, maritime equipment, advanced rail, new materials, and advanced agriculture. But it also extends to industries critical to national security and defense, raw materials and critical minerals, and sectors where China has already used the 90 Percent Model to achieve dangerous dominance.

To understand how convergence operates in practice, consider industries that span this full range. From China's offensive targets to existing choke points to America's defensive advantages:

1. **Automobiles:** China dominates EVs and is using the 90 Percent Model to flood global markets. The American Sphere

must rebuild automotive supply chains, battery production, and charging infrastructure within its borders.

2. **Semiconductors:** China cannot build an end to end chip capability without Taiwan's TSMC, the Netherlands' ASML, and US-based Applied Materials. This trio represents generations of IP, tools, and scientific insight. If these three coordinate, they can shut China out for decades. But coordination is the key.
3. **Critical Minerals:** China controls rare earths, lithium, graphite, and processing capacity. The American Sphere must secure alternative sources from Canada, Greenland, Latin America, Australia, and build refining facilities at home. At the same time, China's processing of these materials depends on inputs controlled by the American Sphere—specialty chemicals, precision equipment, and advanced refining technologies. These reverse choke points can disrupt China's mineral processing and manufacturing supply chains.
4. **Pharmaceuticals:** China produces the majority of the world's active pharmaceutical ingredients. The American Sphere must rebuild production capacity for essential medicines, especially antibiotics, antivirals, and cancer treatments.
5. **Chemicals:** China dominates the global production of base chemicals and specialty intermediates. Critical inputs like dyes, solvents, and polymers vital to industry and defense.

But China's refineries require some advanced catalysts, precision additives, and processing equipment controlled by the American Sphere. The Sphere must secure these reverse choke points while coordinating investment to rebuild chemical production capacity within allied borders.

6. **Telecom:** Huawei and ZTE dominate global infrastructure. The American Sphere must phase out Chinese equipment and build trusted alternatives led by Ericsson, Nokia, and emerging players.

These six industries demonstrate the principles of convergence in action. But they are not the only battlegrounds. The same approach applies across all 10 *Made in China 2025* industries and wherever else China has built dominance through the 90 Percent Model—whether in batteries, solar panels, or advanced manufacturing equipment. The American Sphere must coordinate its response across the full spectrum.

This means:

- **Coordinated action** across the American Sphere, not fragmented national responses.
- **Shared investment** in industrial capacity, technology protection, and supply-chain reconstruction.
- **Unified standards and policies** that prevent China from dividing allies.

- **A clear timeline** to reduce dependence on China's supply chains within three to five years.

The specifics of how this works—the machinery, the coordination mechanisms, the timelines—come in Part III. What matters here is understanding why it's necessary and what's at stake.

WHAT MUST CHANGE

For convergence to work, Trump must shift his approach. He has been operating bilaterally—pressuring each ally individually, negotiating country by country, and using tariffs as leverage on friend and foe alike. That approach has created enormous friction. It has rattled partners whose support is vital.

Trump must now move from **bilateral to multilateral**. He must bring the leadership of the six economic powers together. Not in a forum. Not in a summit. But in a **working coalition** with shared goals, coordinated policies, and a single-minded focus on China.

But first, he must solve his focus problem. Trump has too many **domestic digressions**—political battles, media wars, secondary policy fights. China, Russia, and building this allied convergence should consume 50 percent of his presidential time. Even Iran's nuclear program is secondary compared to breaking the 90 Percent Model.

Focus, focus, focus on China alone. The enemy is China. The goal is to break the 90 Percent Model. The American Sphere must align around that priority.

The leadership of the six powers must come together and say: We will align our tariffs, rebuild our industries, protect our technologies, and reduce our dependence on China. We will do it together. We will do it with urgency. And we will not fracture under pressure.

This is not permanent protectionism. This is a **targeted, time-bound action** to restore fairness and rebuild resilience.

THE LONG GAME

Let me be clear about what lies ahead. This will be a long game. The economic war is not a single confrontation, but a series of skirmishes fought through tariffs, sanctions, technology choke points, and the winning or losing of allies.

Over time, both sides will discover and refine weapons to contain the other. The contest will stretch for years, even decades, until both are forced to recognize the limits of escalation. Only then, after a long grind, might they settle into a fragile equilibrium where neither can dominate, but neither dares to collapse the system. That point is far ahead. Until then, this fight will define the era.

Several scenarios are possible:

- China escalates militarily—via Taiwan blockades, cyberattacks, or South China Sea provocations.

- China plays conciliatory, adjusting the RMB, buying US goods, offering cosmetic reforms—tactics to protect the 90 Percent Model.
- The US escalates financially, freezing assets or delisting Chinese firms, pushing Beijing into deeper surveillance and repression.

All these scenarios are plausible. And every company must now build its own response. Because the next move is coming.

WHY THIS WILL WORK

Convergence has one decisive advantage: **scale**. The six-power bloc commands $60 trillion in GDP. That is more than twice China's sphere. It is home to the deepest capital markets, the most advanced technology, the most productive workers, and the most trusted institutions.

When this bloc aligns, it reshapes the rules of global trade. When it coordinates investment and blocks Chinese dumping in unison, it rebuilds industrial capacity faster than China can flood markets. When it sets technology standards, it decides what the future looks like.

China cannot compete with that. Not over time. Not sustainably. President Xi knows this. That is why he is working so hard to fracture the alliance before it forms.

The question is: Will the American Sphere come together? Will the leaders of these six powers put aside short-term frictions and focus on the long-term threat? Will they coordinate policies with the same discipline they have shown in military alliances?

I believe they can. I believe they must. Because the alternative is the eclipse of the free world's economic power and the rise of an autocratic system that does not share our values, does not respect our institutions, and will not stop until it has reshaped the global order in its image.

But let's be clear about what convergence requires. This is a contest between Trump and Xi, between two systems. And there is no single tool that will win it. Tariffs alone won't break the 90 Percent Model. Neither will currency pressure alone, nor export controls alone.

America and its allies learned a hard lesson when China threatened to cut off magnet supplies. A pain no country can bear. That is the weapon for which the Western world does not yet have a corresponding response. To counteract it, **America and allies must create a package** that makes Beijing understand: if exercised, their threshold of pain will be such that they are willing to negotiate in good faith and accept reciprocal arrangements.

What will work is the coordinated package. Tariffs that protect rebuilding industries. Currency alignment that removes China's structural advantage. Export controls that deny critical inputs. Financial pressure through payment systems. Allied coordination that prevents China from picking off countries one by one. And critically, control of supplies, technology, and other means that can knock out the 90 Percent Model itself.

WHAT COMES NEXT

Convergence is the answer. But convergence is not self-executing. It requires leadership, coordination, and a detailed playbook for how to implement it across industries, governments, and companies.

In Part III of this book, we will deep dive into that execution. The **Convergence Playbook** will show you how governments must coordinate, how industries must rebuild, and how companies must extricate from China and realign within the American Sphere.

But first, we turn to the evidence that this shift is already beginning. Not just in policy, not just in diplomacy, but in the boardrooms and factories where the real fight is being waged.

In the next chapter, we will examine the companies that are already breaking up with China. The CEOs who saw the risk early and acted. The exits that are succeeding. And the lessons they offer for those who must follow.

Because convergence is not just a government strategy. It is a business imperative. And the companies that move first will shape the future.

Chapter 11

The China Breakup

Convergence is the answer. Industrial coordination across the American Sphere. The six-power bloc aligning policies, rebuilding capacity, and breaking China's 90 Percent Model. That is the strategy. That is what must happen.

But strategy without proof is just theory. And the proof is already here. Not in policy papers. Not in diplomatic summits. But in boardrooms, on factory floors, and in the decisions CEOs are making right now.

Companies across the American Sphere are breaking up with China. Some by choice. Others by force. But the pattern is unmistakable. **The great unwinding** has begun. And the leaders who moved early are showing the rest how it can be done.

This chapter is about those leaders. The ones who saw the risk before it became a crisis. Who acted when action was costly. Who protected their core assets and found new paths to growth. Their

stories are not just case studies. They are proof that extrication is possible. And they offer lessons for those who must follow.

DAVID'S DECISION: COURAGE UNDER PRESSURE

I begin with the story of David, CEO of TechCore, a US tech company whose products span communications, surveillance, and integrated systems for industrial and government clients. Like most, they entered China in the 2000s with expectations of market growth. The logic was straightforward: Access a massive market, build local partnerships, and scale revenue.

But as CEO, David became uneasy about something others ignored—the risk of losing control over their most valuable asset: intellectual property.

China was no longer just a market. It was a threat. Chinese startups were entering the field, sometimes luring TechCore employees away with salary offers double what they earned in the US. One competitor actually set up shop right outside TechCore's US headquarters to poach talent. David knew what was coming. The CCP's playbook was becoming clear: lure, extract, replace.

By 2013, he made a quiet but decisive move. He withdrew from the Chinese market.

This was not a panic decision. David had vetted it with his board. He laid out the risks: IP leakage, technology transfer, and the likelihood that within five years, a subsidized Chinese competitor would emerge and undercut TechCore globally. The board endorsed his logic.

When David pulled out, revenues dropped by 12 percent the next year. The stock took a hit. Analysts questioned the decision. Some investors grew restless. But David and his board never stopped communicating. They explained the risk the company had avoided. They showed the new path for growth. They redirected resources to markets where TechCore could compete on merit, not subsidies. And they protected the company's core technology.

The company didn't just rebound, it soared. Market capitalization grew sixfold over the following years. No critical technology was leaked. No core value lost. TechCore emerged stronger, more focused, and more resilient.

But the story doesn't end there. Despite David's exit, Chinese competitors had still managed to take some technology through former employees, leaked designs, or reverse engineering. David filed a lawsuit, and he won. TechCore finally secured its freedom from Chinese infringement, validated by a legal judgment that confirmed what David had known all along: staying in China meant losing control.

David's story teaches one lesson above all: **Leadership is about seeing the risk before it becomes a crisis**. And having the courage to act even when the short-term cost is real.

MNC'S PIVOT: FINDING GROWTH BEYOND CHINA

The second story is MNC, an agricultural supplier that initially bet big on China as a growth engine, only to discover that survival and success required pulling back and adjusting its strategy entirely.

They had entered China through joint ventures, built plants, and introduced base products appropriate for China's small farms. The reasoning was sound: As farms consolidated, they would become ripe for MNC's tech-driven, high-end equipment—AI-powered systems, robotics, and software integration that increased yields and reduced costs.

But China didn't change the way they expected. The farms stayed small. And a crop of competitors sprang up. Subsidized, state-owned, the Chinese players copied MNC's low-end products and even imitated the brand.

Soon the CCP began pressuring MNC to share the edge that differentiated them: the AI, robotics, and software integration that made their high-end equipment superior. MNC faced a choice: Hand over the technology and become irrelevant, or exit and rebuild elsewhere.

A new CEO sized up the situation. The Chinese market wasn't viable for its full product line, and the company could not allow its proprietary technology to leak. He cut his losses and turned his focus and resources to Brazil and India.

In Brazil, large farms adopted MNC's tech fast. The market fit was perfect. India became both a market and a manufacturing hub. Today, 90 percent of MNC's midrange equipment is made there. Because of the change in product mix, the company earns higher profits on lower volume. And there are no viable Chinese competitors threatening its position.

Shifting strategy is never easy. But that's what real leadership demands. MNC faced the facts and acted decisively. Not when it was convenient, but when it was necessary. The company is stronger because of it.

MNC's story teaches another lesson: **Extrication is not retreat. It is repositioning.** Finding markets where you can compete on your terms, not theirs. Where you can build a new global strategy and eliminate China dependence. MNC could do this because China lags far behind in the agricultural innovations that drive farmer productivity. That IP gap is real and sustainable.

JIM'S CHOICE: WHEN VALUES AND STRATEGY ALIGN

Sometime over the December 2022 holidays, I was a houseguest of the founder and CEO of one of the world's largest privately held companies. Dinner concluded. Jim and I retired to his private study for a nightcap. These are the moments when one shares his inner thoughts or anxieties with a trusted person.

Jim said: *"I and my family are scratching our heads. China is our second-largest market, and it's very profitable. Twenty-five percent of our revenues come from there. We are a family company, and we manage with family values. My father built it that way some 60 years ago."*

Here he began to mince words and speak in a low tone. *"The CCP is demanding things that go against our values. They want us to do a joint venture with someone. Take a price reduction. They've broached the topic of state-owned enterprise participation in some way, such as 5 percent equity ownership."*

"Yes, we can stay there. But should we? Or should we start gradually phasing out? It will hurt our scale, our brand, and cash generation. Even worse, I have no doubt if we were to exit, they would conscript our brand and probably compete against us globally. You know too well that they will do anything to dominate global sectors—use subsidies, currency parity advantage, and the like."

We closed the evening by agreeing to meet for breakfast. The next day was Sunday. We slept late and had a cordial brunch. When I left for the airport, Jim was still feeling the weight of his dilemma. During brunch, he had asked me dozens of questions—about timing, how others had navigated a slow exit, and whether there were viable growth markets outside China. He was already thinking about reallocating his resources, even if it meant a hit to margins in the short term.

When Jim and I touched base again shortly thereafter, he had decided he had no choice but to pull out of China. He simply could not reconcile the values of the CCP and those of his family business. The company would take a hit, but it would adapt and survive.

Jim's story is not unique. American and European companies have been allowed to succeed in China only until they have handed over the tools to build their own executioner.

Jim's story teaches a third lesson: **Sometimes the decision to exit is not just strategic; it's moral.** When a market demands you compromise core values, the only path forward is out.

APPLE'S FORESIGHT: BUILDING RESILIENCE AT SCALE

The stories of TechCore, MNC, and Jim show how decisive exits, even under pressure, can protect core assets and create new growth paths. Apple's journey adds another dimension: **foresight**. Apple anticipated the risks and moved early, proving that strategic hedging can be as powerful as bold withdrawal.

Apple's path out of China was not reactive. It was planned. It began quietly, long before headlines made the risks obvious.

I believe Tim Cook likely started scenario planning around 2011 or 2012, when it was clear Xi Jinping would take full control of the CCP. Apple's internal teams were asked to look beyond China, not to abandon it, but to hedge. By 2017, Apple's first plant in India was operational. That timeline tells you everything. Negotiating land, recruiting and training talent, building supplier ecosystems—this is work that takes years.

India stood out for several reasons. A large, trainable, English-speaking workforce. Political alignment with the US. A government ready to support foreign investment with incentives and infrastructure. Apple's supply-chain leader, Sabih Khan (promoted to COO in July 2005), played a pivotal role in identifying the right regions, particularly in the south, and executing with quiet precision.

Today, the **results** speak for themselves:[129]

- Between April and October 2024, Apple produced $10 billion in iPhones from India, a 37 percent increase over the prior year.
- Of that, $7 billion was exported.
- The Production-Linked Incentive (PLI) program supported this growth.
- Apple's ecosystem has created 175,000 direct jobs in India, 72 percent of which are held by women.

India is now more than a supply base. Apple is investing in retail, adapting price points, and producing locally for local demand. At the same time, Apple is also investing over $500 billion in the US. This is not about leaving America. It's about building a resilient global strategy.

Apple's pivot to India was further validated when revenues in China began to decline in 2016. Had Apple not made the move, the financial impact would have been far worse. Potentially unsustainable for its stock price. Cook's early decisions were bold and wise.

Apple didn't fully decouple from China, but it made a strategic reduction. China's contribution to Apple's total revenue has dropped from roughly 25 percent in 2015 to approximately 17 percent in 2024. India will be a reliable partner. If the US chip supply to China is cut off entirely, Apple will still have a base.

Apple's story teaches a fourth lesson: **Resilience is built through diversification and foresight**. The companies that plan for risk before it materializes are the ones that survive when the crisis hits.

THE BROADER WAVE: VALIDATION, NOT COINCIDENCE

These four stories—TechCore, MNC, Jim, and Apple—are not isolated cases. They are early signals of a broader wave now building across industries and geographies.

In Chapter 9, you saw evidence of businesses shifting stance, reallocating capital, and rethinking China exposure. But let me be clear: What we are witnessing is not a series of unrelated decisions. It is a systematic reassessment of risk driven by the same forces these four leaders recognized early.

The exits are accelerating. The wave is widening.

In April 2025, Chinese authorities blacklisted US drone companies like Skydio and BRINC Drones, effectively forcing them out and accelerating their diversification to other markets.

In November 2025, Starbucks announced it was selling control of its China operations, its second-largest market globally, marking one of the most visible exits by a major consumer brand from China to date. This was part of a $4 billion deal to transfer a 60 percent stake to Boyu Capital, leaving Starbucks with a minority share and ongoing licensing rights.[130]

According to a 2024 East & Partners report, more than 50 percent of corporates across Asia, Australia, the UK, and the US have either already moved operations out of China or plan to do so within the next 12 months.[131] The pattern is clear: The risks have outweighed the rewards, and boardrooms are acting. The leaders who move now are the ones who will define the next era.

And the pressure is escalating, validating why leaders like David, MNC's CEO, Jim, and Tim Cook moved early.

Companies are no longer just navigating a market. They are operating inside a geopolitical battleground, **caught in the crossfire**, forced to answer to two masters. US policy has moved beyond tariffs to include outbound investment restrictions, export controls, and secondary sanctions. China has responded with retaliatory tariffs, mineral restrictions, and license suspensions.

Micron is a textbook example. The US restricted advanced chip exports. China retaliated, branding Micron a *"security threat."*

Micron found itself under investigation, barred from key markets, and forced to reconsider its China exposure entirely. Google and Apple are now facing similar heat. As of summer 2025, neither side is backing down.

Those who waited are now being forced to choose. The companies that moved early did so on their own terms. The ones moving now are doing so under fire.

Some companies are redirecting resources without fanfare. Others are being forced out by blacklists, regulatory harassment, or rule changes. Regardless of the trigger, the result is the same. The great unwinding has begun.

WHAT THESE STORIES PROVE

These exits prove three things:

First, extrication is possible. It is painful. It requires courage, capital, and time. But it can be done. And most companies will face it. The companies that do it early, on their own terms, come out stronger.

Second, new growth markets exist. India, Brazil, Southeast Asia, and the American Sphere itself offer scale, talent, and opportunity. The global economy is not China or nothing. There are alternatives. And they are viable.

Third, leadership matters more than ever. The CEOs who saw the risk early—David, MNC's leader, Jim, and Tim Cook—protected their companies. They took short-term hits to secure long-term resilience. That is what real leadership looks like in this moment.

But these stories also reveal a gap. Most companies are still stuck. Not because they don't see the risk. But because they don't know how to move. They don't have a playbook for extrication. They don't know where to find growth. They don't understand how to break free from the choke holds China still controls.

That is what Part III of this book is about.

WHAT COMES NEXT

Part II has shown you three things: America's arsenal, the tide turning, and the case for convergence. You have seen the strengths America holds. You have seen the evidence that change is beginning. And you have seen why convergence—industrial coordination across the American Sphere—is the only way to break China's 90 Percent Model.

Now you have seen proof that this is not just theory. Companies are already acting. Leaders are already moving. The exits are real. The results are measurable. And the lesson is clear: **This can be done**.

But knowing it can be done is not the same as knowing how to do it. That requires execution. Detailed, coordinated, disciplined execution across governments, industries, and companies.

Part III delivers that execution.

First, **the Convergence Playbook**. How governments and industries must coordinate to rebuild capacity, align policies, and break China's choke hold. The strategic fronts. The mechanisms. The timeline. The leadership required.

Then, **the Business Extrication Playbook**. How companies can safely disentangle from China, find new growth markets, and rebuild resilience. The steps. The risks. The hard choices boards and CEOs must make.

These are not abstract strategies. They are operational playbooks. Built for speed. Built for scale. Built to win.

The tide is turning. Convergence is the answer. And the proof is already here. Now it is time to execute.

PART III

Counterattack: Urgent, Determined, Coordinated

Chapter 12

The Convergence Playbook

You have seen China's strategy. You know America's strengths. You understand why convergence is the answer. And you have seen proof that companies are already moving, breaking free from China's grip and finding new paths to growth.

Now comes **execution**.

It is easy to propose strategies. It is harder to propose actions that work. America's response to China has failed for a decade, giving President Xi an advantage he now believes is insurmountable. He assumes the West will never develop a cogent approach. That assumption must be proven wrong.

Over the 60 years of working with the world's largest corporations—across America, Brazil, China, and Japan—I have proposed only what can be executed. My clients have kept me for tenures ranging from 10 to 40 years because I deliver practical actions, not theories.

What follows is a set of coherent actions. You may find them naive or impossible. Many will point to obstacles. I expect that. But I urge you to consider: **What is the alternative to what has not worked?** Leaders must find the gaps, refine this playbook, and make it more specific. China's march is an existential threat to the American-led economic order.

This is a **call to arms.** You can shoot at this playbook, improve it, or propose something better. But having no cogent approach is what President Xi expects—and that expectation is his greatest asset.

In Chapter 10, I described the **coordinated package** that creates a threshold of pain for Beijing. Pain severe enough that they are forced to negotiate. This chapter shows you how to build and deploy it.

This is the playbook. The machinery of convergence. How the six-power bloc—the United States, the European Union, Japan, South Korea, Israel, and the United Kingdom—must coordinate policies, align investments, and rebuild industrial capacity at scale. How governments must operate. How businesses must be supported. And how the free world can break China's 90 Percent Model within three to five years.

These six powers anchor the American Sphere, but they do not stand alone. Taiwan, Canada, Australia, India, and others form a broader ecosystem. What matters is that the core six set the standards, coordinate the policies, and lead with clarity. Others will follow. The strength is in the center of gravity, not in rigid membership lists.

Convergence is not a summit. It is not a declaration. **It is an operating system.** Built for speed. Built for coordination. Built to win.

This chapter shows you how it works.

THE COORDINATION MACHINERY

Convergence means three things coming together: allies coordinating policies, governments supporting business, and the public understanding what is at stake.

Without that alignment, policies fragment. Investments scatter. Execution stalls. That is what has plagued the West's response to China for two decades.

No more.

This playbook shows what must be built, how allies must work together, and what support businesses need. Each part must move with speed and discipline.

Department of Manufacturing and Advanced Technology: The National Command Center

Every country in the American Sphere must create a **Department of Manufacturing and Advanced Technology**. Not buried inside Commerce or Treasury, but independent. Singular in focus. Modeled on the creation of Homeland Security after 9/11.

The Commerce Department's Investment Accelerator Unit is a good first step. Led by Michael Grimes, a veteran investment banker, it is fast-tracking projects over $1 billion and cutting regulatory delays. But the Investment Accelerator is built for deals. Its team of lawyers, bankers, and regulatory specialists can move capital—but they cannot think four moves ahead. They cannot design the coordinated package of tariffs, currency tools, export controls, and reverse choke holds that this fight requires.

What is needed is something closer to how Xi operates. As described in Chapter 2, Xi chairs more than a dozen LSGs that cut across ministries and bypass formal bureaucracy. These groups bring data directly to Xi, propose options, and enable him to make decisions that last a decade. Nothing strategic moves without his nod. The Department of Manufacturing and Advanced Technology must function with the same cross-cutting authority and strategic depth.

This department must be headed by a globally recognized CEO with context on China. An operator who has built and run businesses at scale, not an investment banker managing deal flow. Leaders like Jeff Immelt (former GE CEO), Jeff Wilke (former Amazon Consumer CEO), Dave Cote (former Honeywell CEO), Andrew Liveris (former Dow Chemical CEO), Ed Breen (former DuPont CEO), Fred Hassan (former Schering-Plough CEO), or John May (John Deere CEO). These are executives who understand manufacturing, supply chains, and China. They know how to execute at scale.

The department must also include a game theorist, someone from business who has applied game theory in practice, not just in academia. The telecom spectrum auctions proved how game-theoretic thinking shapes competitive outcomes. This contest with China is about equilibrium. Anticipating Xi's moves and designing responses that think four steps ahead.

The team must include operators and technical experts: chemical engineers, pharmaceutical scientists, manufacturing specialists, technologists, and experts in primary supplier ecosystems. These are the skills needed to understand reverse choke holds, design industrial policy, and execute at the speed this moment demands.

This department's mandate is clear: Rebuild and advance domestic manufacturing and advanced technology. Coordinate across federal agencies and state governments. Align policy with global partnerships. And send a powerful signal to allies, markets, and competitors: We are acting.

In the US, this means appointing a secretary of manufacturing and advanced technology with cabinet-level authority. Every state should follow suit, appointing its own state-level manufacturing leader and a team of experts to support them. Governors can negotiate directly with global partners. States can compete or collaborate to attract investment, just as they do today for companies like Amazon or Tesla.

India is already doing this. Prime Minister Modi has unlocked competitive fire among Indian states. Gujarat and Tamil Nadu now compete to attract foreign direct investment, mirroring national goals with local precision. American states can and should do the same.

Every embassy in the free world should have a **Manufacturing and Advanced Technology Attaché**. Every member of the American Sphere should mirror this structure. The world has a manufacturing hole. And we must fill it, together.

The War Room: Operating at the Speed of Crisis

Washington cannot execute bureaucracy as usual. Execution must run at the speed of competition. With the clarity and intensity of a national war room.

This war room must:

- **Recruit elite talent** from government, academia, and industry. The sharpest operators, not the best bureaucrats.
- **Model the future relentlessly.** Running simulations, stress-testing strategies, and preparing for every move Beijing might make.
- **Exploit real-time data.** Leveraging AI and large language models to process trade, financial, and industrial flows as they happen.
- **Understand the adversary.** Integrating psychological profiles of rival leaders into decision-making and predicting the opponents' moves.

Its output must feed directly to the highest levels of policy, with two nonnegotiables: It transcends presidential terms, and it stays bipartisan. The stakes demand no less.

The rhythm must change. Replace ceremonial meetings with short, high-intensity sessions where top policymakers operate from one shared set of facts, fuse economic and military intelligence into unified strategies, and rehearse responses through simulations that leave no blind spots.

This must be a **living operating system** for national security. Always adapting. Always ready. Built to win.

And what Washington builds, every ally must mirror. Japan, the EU, South Korea, Israel, and the UK must create their own war rooms. Together, these nodes form a network. **Shared operating hubs** that coordinate investments, align standards across sectors, and share real-time data on supply chains, security risks, and market movements.

The hole China filled was one we created through complacency and underinvestment. We can close it through global coordination that operationalizes speed: joint task forces meeting with the urgency of a crisis, data flowing in real time, and decisions made as if survival depends on them.

Treasury and Commerce Umbrella: Supporting Business

Governments alone cannot rebuild industrial capacity. Businesses must lead. But they cannot do it without support.

That is why every country in the American Sphere must create a **Treasury and Commerce umbrella** for businesses operating within the convergence framework. The umbrella must coordinate with the Department of Manufacturing and Advanced Technology to respond quickly to Chinese export actions—dumping, subsidies, and restrictions. This is not subsidies like China's. This is support to help American companies compete and rebuild.

Here is what it looks like:

- **Tax incentives and relief.** Tax cuts that make it easier for firms to carry the burden of tariffs and higher input costs. Trump's approach in the US—his "big beautiful bill" saving businesses around $100 billion—is one example. Other countries must follow suit.
- **Low-cost loans and capital access.** Financing for companies relocating production, building new facilities, or diversifying supply chains. The Small Business Administration's Made in America Manufacturing Initiative is a start. It must scale.
- **Price protection mechanisms.** India's Goods and Services Tax relief program offers a model worth studying. When its businesses faced tariff pressures, the government provided domestic tax adjustments to cushion the impact. This kind of creative support helps businesses absorb transition costs while they diversify away from Chinese suppliers.
- **Regulatory relief.** Cutting red tape, fast-tracking permits, and removing barriers that slow execution. The goal: Ease $100 bil-

lion worth of regulatory burdens across the American Sphere within two years.

This umbrella must extend across all six economic powers. Coordinated. Aligned. So that a company operating in the US, Germany, or South Korea receives similar support and faces similar expectations. The objective is clear: Reduce dependence on China's supply chains within **three to five years.**

This is painful. This is difficult. But it must be done. And with the right support, it can be done. Within 12 months, psychology shifts. Pain becomes confidence. Businesses see progress and momentum builds.

THE SEVEN DOMAINS OF CONVERGENCE

With the machinery in place, convergence must execute across seven critical domains. Each is interlocked. Progress in one demands movement in the rest. Together, they form the map for how the American Sphere regains control of the fight.

1. Currency Alignment

Tariffs alone will not achieve a zero-trade deficit. Without currency realignment, America and its allies will continue to bleed hard currency to countries running large surpluses—China, Mexico, Vietnam, and even allies like Japan and Germany within the American Sphere itself.

Let me be clear: Convergence does not mean every imbalance disappears overnight. **Some adjustment is required even among trusted partners.** Trade surplus correction and currency parity alignment must happen within the Sphere, not just against China. The difference is **intent.** Within the American Sphere, realignment strengthens all parties. With China, **it is about survival.**

The trade imbalance is fueled by currency misalignment. Most of these nations have used exchange rates as weapons, undervaluing their currencies to make exports artificially cheap and build strategic reserves. They have abused this privilege for decades.

There is no economic theory that solves this. The last major realignment was the **Plaza Accord in 1985**. That was four decades ago. The imbalance has only widened since. We need another realignment, urgently.

The only real lever is tariffs. And when applied at scale, they force currencies to appreciate. We are already seeing it. Between October 2024 and October 2025, Taiwan's dollar appreciated by nearly 8 percent against the US dollar. As the currencies of these trade-surplus nations strengthen, their interest costs fall relative to the US, giving them more room to invest at home.

Tariffs plus currency appreciation begin to restore price levels to where they should be. That shift draws more capital into those economies, even as investment flows into America itself. The downside is some inflationary pressure in the US, driven both by currency effects and rising domestic investment. But growth should remain solid.

We have seen this work before. Singapore's deliberate currency strengthening over decades made the country more expensive but forced it to move up the value chain. As Lee Kuan Yew described, Singapore accepted short-term pain to build a high-income, innovation-led economy.

America must now demand similar realignment from surplus nations—China, Japan, Mexico, and others—backed by clear public communication and political resolve. The Federal Reserve will cooperate, managing rates to support the transition. The public must understand what is at stake. There will be temporary inflation. Slower growth. Global pushback. But the alternative is the long-term erosion of our sovereignty.

Currency realignment is the foundation. Without it, the rest of this playbook becomes difficult to implement, and China's 90 Percent Model remains intact.

2. Manufacturing and Supply-Chain Reconstruction

Supply chain is manufacturing. And manufacturing is national power.

This domain is not only about moving factories. It is about reclaiming control over the arteries of global trade. From ports to data cables, from shipping lanes to logistics systems—every layer must be secured.

America has begun to respond. In 2025, a consortium led by BlackRock acquired both ends of the Panama Canal for $22.8 billion.[132] This was not a business deal. It was a strategic win to block Chinese leverage over a critical maritime passage. The bipartisan Ships for America Act builds on this by funding domestic shipbuilding, imposing new port fees on Chinese vessels, and creating a Maritime Security Trust Fund.

But this must go further. It must be surgical and fast:

- **Rewiring undersea cables.** Data sovereignty is national security.
- **Blocking backdoor exports.** Much of what we import from Vietnam and Mexico is made in Chinese-owned factories. These transshipments must be stopped.
- **Reviving shipbuilding.** America needs this capacity back. Without it, control of sea trade routes slips away.

And above all, we must manufacture again.

America already has the seeds of industrial revival. Advanced manufacturing firms like Protolabs, FANUC, Fabco-Air, and select Tesla and Siemens lines prove America's edge still exists.

Take Protolabs as a concrete example (see Exhibit 29: mother factory[133]). It represents the *"mother factory"* model—a digital production platform that turns design into finished parts in hours, not weeks. I have visited their facility: **high-precision, lights-out**

manufacturing, no Chinese equipment. Fully capable of serving Amazon, Tesla, and major industrial companies.

This is how we can rapidly scale precision manufacturing locally, reducing dependence on overseas supply chains. With the right support—low-cost loans, protected pricing, clear incentives—they can be scaled nationally.

Exhibit 29: Protolabs: The "Mother Factory" of America's Manufacturing Renaissance

Protolabs is a breakthrough example of America's capability to leapfrog China in manufacturing. It is a "Mother Factory"—a digital manufacturing platform that not only produces parts but enables the rapid creation of new	While much of the world outsourced production and fell into dependency on China, Protolabs quietly built the infrastructure and digital capability to manufacture at home—fast, precise, and at scale.	With a fully integrated digital thread, it collapses production cycles from weeks to hours, making custom, precise parts available within a day. This capability positions it as a cornerstone of the American industrial resurgence.

Source: Author's analysis and field visit

What Makes Protolabs a "Mother Factory"

Feature	Impact
Digital Twin Technology	Creates virtual replicas of components before production, reducing error and cycle time.
One-Day Manufacturing Capability	Delivers custom parts within 24 hours— a global first.
Software-Driven Automation	No human machinists; end to end instructions are generated by algorithms and robotics.
Two-Pronged Fulfilment Model	Combines owned digital factories with a digitally enabled global manufacturing network.
Precision & Scale	Used by Fortune 500s for both prototyping and scaled production with no minimum order size.
Zero Dependency on China	Equipment sourced from the US, Japan, and Germany—no reliance on Chinese tech or supply chain.
Factory Builder	Capable of producing core components that enable other companies to rapidly launch full factories.

This is not just a factory. It's a factory that can build other factories. It is a strategic asset in the race to reclaim manufacturing dominance.

Source: Author's analysis and field visit

CHAPTER 12

Protolabs Facilities

CNC facility (interior)

3DP facility (exterior)

IM facility (exterior)

CNC milling process

3DP facility (interior)

IM cobot automation

SM forming

3DP (DMLS) process

IM CMM quality control

Source: Author's analysis and field visit

The focus must be strategic. Where China has built dominance through the 90 Percent Model—automobiles, semiconductors, critical minerals, pharmaceuticals, chemicals, telecom—the American Sphere must coordinate its response. This is selective self-sufficiency at scale. Not rebuilding everything, but securing the choke points that matter most.

To achieve this, the US, EU, Japan, South Korea, Israel, and the UK must coinvest, share standards, and align incentives to create a secure production base outside of China. This is how supply chains are rewired, with coordinated capital and execution.

Rebuilding industrial muscle at this scale requires bold financing. America has done this before. The Marshall Plan rebuilt postwar Europe with $13 billion (over $150 billion today). The Troubled Asset Relief Program stabilized financial markets with $700 billion during the 2008 crisis. It was temporary, targeted, and ultimately recouped.

The same principle applies now. A temporary but decisive industrial financing plan, aligned with allies, can rebuild resilience and end dependence on hostile supply chains.

Early sparks are already visible. Tesla, Panasonic, American Giant, Walmart, Siemens, Honda, Intel, Micron, Asahi—all are investing in US-based production. The manufacturing revival is centered on semiconductors, EVs and batteries, advanced electronics, and consumer goods. The geographic hotspots are the Southwest, Midwest, Southeast, upstate New York, Idaho, and California.

But this is only the beginning. This revival must scale—faster, broader, and in coordination with allies—so that every investment strengthens the larger goal: reducing the trade deficit, regaining control over choke points, and rebuilding industrial depth.

3. Reverse Choke Holds: The Hidden Leverage

Everyone talks about China's choke hold on critical minerals. Rare earths. Lithium. Graphite. The materials that power modern industry. And yes, China controls much of that processing capacity. But there is another story. One that almost no one is telling.

China's processing operations depend on inputs from the American Sphere. Small-dollar imports. Specialty chemicals. Precision equipment. Ultra-pure materials. Without them, China's refineries, fabrication plants, and manufacturing complexes cannot operate.

This is the reverse choke hold. And it is the most underutilized leverage the American Sphere possesses.

The Hidden Asymmetry

How did I find this? I drilled down. Layer by layer. Supply chain by supply chain.

Take China's rare earth magnet industry. That's supply chain one. The suppliers to those magnet factories, that's supply chain two. Their suppliers are supply chain three. Keep going. By the time you reach supply chain four and five, you find the inputs that make everything above possible: ultra-pure chemicals, specialty acids, precision materials.

No country has all these chemicals. None. And when you drill down to the HS code (the global customs classification that tracks every product crossing every border) level—electronic-grade hydrochloric acid (2806.10), high-purity nitric acid (2808.00), specialty fluoropolymers (3904.61), nuclear-grade ion-exchange resins (3914.00)—a pattern emerges. **Most of these inputs come from America and its allies.**

Here is what makes this powerful: $10–40 million import line can control $10–20 billion of Chinese industrial output.

A note on numbers: *The dollar figures that follow are directional estimates based on trade data, customs records, and industry analysis. Actual import values fluctuate with market conditions, and precise breakdowns by purity grade or end-use application are often obscured in customs classifications. What matters is not the exact dollar amount, but the strategic reality: Small-value imports with no viable substitutes can control enormous downstream industrial capacity. The leverage ratio—$10–40 million controlling $10–20 billion of output—is the key insight, not the precision of individual line items.*

Take rare earth processing. China dominates global refining capacity. Over 90 percent of the world's rare earth processing happens in China. But those refineries require inputs China cannot produce domestically at the required purity levels.

Without these inputs from Japan, South Korea, the US, and Europe, China's rare earth processing operations degrade or halt. And rare earths feed into magnets, catalysts, phosphors, and defense systems worth tens of billions of dollars annually.

Here are the specific choke points:

Electronic-grade hydrochloric acid: China imports approximately $14 million annually from Japan, South Korea, and other Asian suppliers. This acid is critical for clean leaching, re-leaching, and powder cleaning stages. If specific grades (electronic/ultrapure) disappear, rare earth output cannot meet export purity standards or fabrication specifications. The refineries can run, but the product becomes worthless for advanced applications.

High-purity nitric acid and hydrofluoric acid: China imports $20–35 million annually. These are used in oxidative leaching and impurity removal. Plants cannot substitute lower-grade alternatives without fouling solvent extraction circuits and corroding equipment. The result: reduced throughput, increased downtime, and degraded output quality.

Specialty fluoropolymers (PTFE and advanced grades): China imports $80–90 million of high-specification fluoropolymers. These materials line solvent extraction plants, providing seals, gaskets, and corrosion-resistant surfaces. Loss of certain high-spec grades leads to more leaks, safety limits, and throughput cuts. A few tens of millions in imports protect hundreds of millions in processing capacity.

Ion-exchange resins (nuclear and rare earth grades): China's total resin imports are approximately $230 million annually from the EU, US, Japan, and South Korea. But only a fraction, perhaps $10–20 million, goes to rare earth applications. That small slice determines whether polishing and high-purity circuits can function. Without the right resins, final product purity collapses.

High-spec organophosphorus extractants: A single extractant compound, like a CYANEX-type or HEHEHP-grade used in solvent extraction circuits, may represent only $5–15 million per year in product flow. But without it, tens of billions of rare earth, nickel, and cobalt capacity suffer yield and purity hits. These extractants are the chemical keys to the entire refining process.

The dollar amounts are small. The impact is massive. Losing $50–180 million in annual imports can degrade or halt $50-plus billion in rare earth value chains and all the downstream industries that depend on them.

This is the hidden asymmetry (see–Exhibit 30: reverse choke holds[134]). China controls the processing. But the American Sphere controls the inputs that make processing possible.

Exhibit 30: Reverse Choke Holds—Small Inputs, Massive Impact

REVERSE CHOKE HOLDS

$10–40M imports →$10–20B output controlled
Small, Coordinated Controls = Massive Strategic Impact

CHINA'S INDUSTRIAL OUTPUT (VALUE CONTROLLED)

Rare Earth Processing
$50B+
Magnets, catalysts, phosphors, defense systems

Semiconductors
$500B+
Chips, electronics, AI systems

Batteries & EVs
$200B+
Electric vehicles, energy storage

Chemicals & Refining
$1T+
Industrial inputs, processed materials

Agriculture & Food
Critical
Processing, livestock production

Depends on American Sphere Inputs

AMERICAN SPHERE INPUTS (IMPORT VALUE)

SHORT TERM (3–6 MONTHS)

- Rare Earth Chemicals
  $50–180M
- Neon Gas
  ~$50M
- EUV Photoresists
  ~$500M
- Electronic-Grade Chemicals
  ~$100M

MEDIUM TERM (6–18 MONTHS)

- Specialty Polymers
  $100–300M
- Industrial Enzymes
  ~$200M
- High-Purity Silicon
  ~$150M
- Specialty Fluoropolymers
  $80–90M

LONG TERM (18–36 MONTHS)

- Animal Genetics
  ~$100M
- Hybrid Seeds
  ~$500M
- Advanced Battery Materials
  $200–400M
- Biotech Intermediates
  ~$300M

Source: Author's analysis

Three Tiers of Leverage

The American Sphere controls inputs across China's entire industrial base. These fall into three tiers based on the timeline to impact:

Short-Term Leverage (3–6 Month Impact)

These inputs stop or severely degrade production almost immediately:

1. Rare Earth Processing Chemicals

As detailed above, China's rare earth refineries depend on ultra-pure chemicals from the American Sphere—electronic-grade acids, specialty fluoropolymers, ion-exchange resins, and organophosphorus extractants. These inputs, totaling approximately $50–180M in annual imports, control over $50 billion in rare earth processing capacity and downstream applications.

Impact: China's rare earth processing efficiency drops 30–50 percent within three to six months. Cannot meet quality standards for export or advanced applications. Tens of billions in downstream industries—magnets for EVs and wind turbines, catalysts for petroleum refining, phosphors for displays and lighting, and defense systems—are affected. Without these inputs, China's choke hold on rare earth processing becomes a choke hold on itself.

2. Semiconductor Production Inputs

- **Neon gas:** 70 percent is supplied from Ukraine, Russia, the US, and Europe. Used in deep ultraviolet lithography lasers. China imports 50–70 percent of its neon needs. Cuts off all advanced semiconductor production within three to six months.
- **EUV photoresists:** JSR (Japan), Shin-Etsu (Japan), and Tokyo Ohka Kogyo (Japan) control 90-plus percent of the global market. Cannot design or manufacture chips below 7nm without these materials. No alternatives exist. Development cycle for alternatives: 10–15 years.
- **Electronic-grade chemicals (for semiconductors):** Ultra-pure hydrochloric acid, hydrofluoric acid, and phosphoric acid. Required for wafer cleaning, etching, and processing. China imports most high-purity grades from Japan, South Korea, and the US.

Impact: Advanced semiconductor fabs shut down within three to six months. Cannot produce AI chips, military processors, 5G equipment, or advanced automotive electronics. The entire technology supply chain collapses.

3. Agricultural Protein Feeds

- **Soybeans:** China imports 100-plus million tons annually from the US (32 percent), Brazil (33 percent), and Argentina (30 percent). Soybeans provide 70 percent of China's protein feed for livestock. Domestic production covers less than 20 percent of needs.
- **Corn (maize):** China imports 20–30 million tons annually, primarily from the US (50–60 percent), Ukraine (20–30 percent), and Brazil (10–20 percent). Used for animal feed and industrial processing.

Impact: Within three to six months, strategic reserves deplete. Forced livestock culling begins. Meat prices spike 50–100 percent or more. Social instability rises (food is China's number-one political priority). Must divert grain from human consumption, causing bread and noodle prices to rise.

Medium-Term Leverage (6–18 Month Impact)

These inputs degrade production quality and industrial efficiency:

1. Refining Catalysts

- **Fluid catalytic cracking (FCC) catalysts:** Grace (US), BASF (Germany), Albemarle (US)
- **Hydroprocessing catalysts:** Johnson Matthey (UK), Criterion (Shell/Haldor Topsoe)

- China's refineries use 40–60 percent imported catalysts for efficiency

Impact: Refinery efficiency drops 15–30 percent. Gasoline and diesel quality degrade. Cannot meet Euro 6 or China 6 emission standards. Military fuel logistics impacted (jet fuel, marine diesel quality suffer).

2. Specialty Polymers

- **Polyimide films:** DuPont (US), Toray (Japan), Kaneka (Japan). Used in flexible displays, 5G antennas, aerospace, and military electronics. China imports 60–70 percent of high-performance grades.
- **High-performance epoxy resins:** Huntsman (US), Hexion (US), Mitsubishi Chemical (Japan). Essential for wind turbine blades, aerospace composites, and PCB substrates. China produces commodity grades but not aerospace/military specifications.

Impact: Cannot scale EV production (battery separators need specialty polymers). Cannot scale wind and solar (epoxy resins for blades and encapsulation). Electronics exports become uncompetitive.

3. Industrial Enzymes

- **Novozymes (Denmark):** 45 percent global market share
- **DuPont Nutrition & Biosciences (US)**
- **DSM (Netherlands)**

- **BASF (Germany)**

Used in textile processing, detergent manufacturing, food processing, biofuel production, and pulp and paper.

Impact: Cannot replicate decades of enzyme engineering. Industrial efficiency drops 20–40 percent. Textile export competitiveness erodes. Food processing scale and efficiency decline.

4. Potash Fertilizers

- China imports 10–12 million tons annually from Canada (Nutrien, Mosaic), Russia/Belarus, Israel (ICL)
- Essential for maintaining crop yields

Impact: Crop yields drop 10–20 percent within two to three years. Food import dependency increases. High-intensity agriculture model becomes unsustainable.

Long-Term Leverage (18-36 Month Impact)

These inputs erode competitiveness and innovation over time:

1. Animal Breeding Genetics

- **Pig breeding stock:** PIC/Genus (UK/US), Topigs Norsvin (Netherlands)
- **Poultry genetics:** Aviagen (US), Cobb-Vantress (US)
- **Dairy cattle genetics:** Alta Genetics (US), CRV (Netherlands)

Impact: Meat production efficiency drops 15–30 percent over three to five years. Feed conversion rates worsen. Cannot maintain current meat consumption without increasing imports or prices.

2. Hybrid Seeds

- **Corn and soybean hybrids:** Corteva (US), Bayer (Germany)
- Hybrid vigor seeds boost yields 20–40 percent compared to conventional varieties
- China's domestic seed varieties are lower-yielding

Impact: Agricultural productivity degrades over time. Must increase land under cultivation or accept lower output. Food self-sufficiency targets become impossible.

3. Pharmaceutical and Biotech Intermediates

- **Cell culture media:** Thermo Fisher (US), Merck (Germany), Sartorius (Germany)
- **Chromatography resins:** Cytiva/GE Healthcare (US/Sweden), Merck (Germany)
- **Single-use bioreactors:** Sartorius (Germany), Thermo Fisher (US)

Impact: Biologics production (monoclonal antibodies, vaccines) severely limited. Cannot produce cutting-edge drugs domestically. Pharmaceutical innovation stalls. Health care system quality degrades.

4. Advanced Battery Materials

- **Electrolyte additives:** Fluorinated solvents from Solvay (Belgium), 3M (US), Central Glass (Japan)
- **High-purity lithium salts ($LiPF_6$):** Stella Chemifa (Japan), Morita Chemical (Japan)
- **Battery separators (high-end):** Asahi Kasei (Japan), Toray (Japan), SK Innovation (South Korea); ceramic-coated separators for safety and performance

Impact: Premium EV production suffers (safety and performance degrade). Cannot compete in high-end global EV markets. Battery overcapacity strategy limited to commodity segments.

Why This Only Works Through Convergence

Here is the critical point: **This leverage only exists if the American Sphere coordinates export controls.**

If the US acts alone, China sources from Europe or Japan. If Europe acts alone, China sources from the US or South Korea. Unilateral action creates arbitrage. China finds workarounds.

This is already happening. In late 2025, Clariant of Switzerland completed a $100 million expansion[135] of its chemical operations in China—specialty chemicals that may well feed into the very supply chains the American Sphere should be controlling. Shareholder value trumping national security. While some nations restrict, others fill the gap. **This is exactly the coordination failure Xi is counting on.**

But when the six powers—United States, European Union, Japan, South Korea, Israel, United Kingdom—coordinate restrictions on specific inputs, **there are no alternatives.**

These materials require:

- Ultra-high purity (99.9999 percent plus in many cases)
- Decades of R&D and process knowledge
- Specialized equipment and quality control systems
- Global supply chains concentrated in the American Sphere

China cannot replicate these quickly. Not in 5 years. Not in 10 years. Some, like advanced photoresists or industrial enzymes, may take 15–20 years to achieve parity even with unlimited funding.

The biological systems (enzymes, animal genetics, hybrid seeds) are even harder. These represent 40-plus years of selective breeding and bioengineering. China would need to start from scratch and compress decades of development into years. It is not impossible. But it is not fast.

The Execution Framework

Reverse choke holds must be executed with precision:

Step 1: Identify the critical nodes

- Ultra-pure chemicals for semiconductors and rare earth processing
- Specialty polymers and catalysts for industrial processes

- Agricultural inputs (soybeans, potash, hybrid seeds, animal genetics)
- Pharmaceutical and biotech precursors

Step 2: Coordinate export controls across the American Sphere

- Not blanket bans—targeted controls on specific purity grades and applications
- Service and maintenance restrictions (equipment degrades without OEM support)
- Tied to end-use verification (block reexport to military or dual-use applications)

Step 3: Synchronize timing

- Phase implementation to create continuous pressure
- Short-term inputs first (immediate impact)
- Medium-term inputs second (cascading degradation)
- Long-term inputs third (strategic erosion)

Step 4: Maintain supplier compliance

- Enforce controls on Western companies (Linde, BASF, Novozymes, JSR, DuPont, etc.)
- Monitor third-party transshipment routes
- Use secondary sanctions if needed to close loopholes

Step 5: Use as negotiation leverage

- Reverse choke holds are not permanent—they are time-bound pressure tools
- Goal: Force China to dismantle the 90 Percent Model
- Relief comes when China agrees to verifiable reforms (currency realignment, subsidy elimination, market access)

The Strategic Impact

Within 6–12 months of coordinated action:

- Advanced semiconductor production degrades or halts
- Rare earth processing efficiency drops, output quality declines
- Food prices spike, forcing increased agricultural imports
- Industrial production costs rise, export competitiveness erodes

Within 12–24 months:

- Technology innovation slows (cannot access cutting-edge materials)
- Manufacturing overcapacity becomes economically unsustainable
- Military modernization constrained (cannot produce reliable advanced systems at scale)
- Economic growth model breaks—forced to negotiate or face internal economic crisis

Knocking out the 90 Percent Model will create **unbearable pain for Xi**. He will resist to the end. But coordinated pressure across all six powers leaves him no escape route. That is the point.

This Is Convergence in Action

Reverse choke holds are not about punishing China. They are about **restoring balance.** About using the leverage the American Sphere already possesses but has never coordinated to deploy.

This is what convergence looks like when executed with precision. Not speeches. Not summits. But coordinated action on specific inputs that control tens of billions of dollars of industrial output.

China built its power on controlling downstream processing. But it remains dependent on upstream inputs it cannot produce at the purity, quality, and scale required for advanced manufacturing. **That dependency is the hidden asymmetry.** And it is the most powerful tool the American Sphere has to break the 90 Percent Model.

The question is not whether this leverage exists. It does. The question is whether the American Sphere has the coordination and discipline to use it.

4. Technology Protection and Innovation Control

Technology is now the terrain of the economic war. The CCP understands this better than anyone. It is pursuing a single-minded goal: Extract, absorb, or replicate American innovation at any cost.

CHAPTER 12

Despite years of effort, Washington has failed to fully plug the leaks. Industrial secrets continue to be siphoned through minority investments, shell companies, academic tie-ups, and talent poaching.

We have reached a point where critical technologies such as AI, semiconductors, quantum computing, and bio-engineering are national security infrastructure. They must be protected as such:

- **Block access** to US labs, IP, and innovation networks for any China-linked entity.
- **Punish any ally or firm** that licenses US-origin tech to CCP-backed entities.
- **Mandate transparency** in tech investments and research affiliations.

The old boundaries are gone. Every dollar of venture capital, every academic tie-up, every supplier relationship must now be scrutinized. If it strengthens the CCP's hand, it weakens ours.

Even allies must play by these rules. If a European company licenses US-origin technology to a Chinese military-linked firm, it should lose privileged access to the US market. Only those who uphold the same standards can be called trusted partners.

At the same time, America must double down on its natural advantage: talent. The best minds in the world still want to come here because America rewards ingenuity and reinvention. China can subsidize factories. But it cannot replicate the creative dynamism of a free society.

That is the magnet. That is the moat. And it must be protected and scaled.

5. Alliance Architecture in Action

Convergence is not an abstract concept. It is the American Sphere operating as a unified bloc.

The six economic powers—US, EU, Japan, South Korea, Israel, UK—must align on three strategic goals:

1. **Rebalance trade.** Achieve zero trade deficit with China through aligned tariffs and targeted measures.
2. **Rebuild capability together.** Relocate manufacturing and supply chains out of China, coinvesting over three to five years to recreate missing capacity inside the Sphere.
3. **Block China's next wave.** Prevent China from achieving the 90 Percent Model in the 10 *Made in China 2025* industries and sectors tied to defense and national security. Deploy coordinated tariffs, investment controls, and technology restrictions NOW—before dominance locks in, not after.
4. **Protect technology and prepare militarily.** Stop export leakage, set shared standards, and ensure readiness against security threats.

Achieving these goals requires a strategy executed with the precision of military coordination. The first phase is hard work: tough love, friction, tariffs, and trade-offs. Every ally must understand that if

China captures the commanding heights of technology, production, and currency, everyone loses.

The second phase is payoff: market access, joint investment, and defense guarantees.

Progress is already visible. The ICE Pact with Canada and Finland. AUKUS is expanding into cyber, AI, and advanced manufacturing. QUAD is moving beyond military drills to include supply chains, critical minerals, and technology standards. The US-India semiconductor corridor linking R&D and manufacturing.

These are early nodes of a network that must now expand with shared tariffs, shared investment banks, and shared digital standards. This is not WTO 2.0. It is a lean, strategic coalition for resilience, designed to withstand a known adversary.

The rule is simple: If you play both sides, you don't get full access. Choose.

6. Communication and Narrative Control

Right now, China looks coordinated, confident, and consistent. President Xi speaks with a single voice. America looks hesitant and divided.

That perception gap is a strategic risk. The US and its allies must speak with discipline and frequency about what we are doing, why it matters, and how it strengthens the free world.

This requires a coordinated effort to:

- **Expose CCP propaganda networks** inside the US and allied countries.
- **Cut off funding and lobbying routes** from Chinese state-backed entities.
- **Create real-time communications** from Washington and allied capitals to clarify what the CCP is doing and why it matters.
- **Mandate transparency** in media, academia, and business on any partnerships or funding links to Chinese government actors.

And above all, we must take the public with us. The strategy must include a domestic campaign. Like a state of war. A daily message. Simple points repeated across TV, podcasts, social media, email, YouTube—everywhere the narrative battle is being fought.

The public must see what is happening and why it matters. They must see results. Jobs returning, factories reopening, tech breakthroughs being protected. And that message must be relentless.

States must play a key role. Governors, local business councils, and state economic agencies must step up. State-level manufacturing leaders must drive coordination, just as they would in a wartime economy, because that's what this is.

Internal cohesion will determine the pace of execution. The CCP is betting we won't get it. That we will remain fragmented, politicized, and distracted. That bet must be proven wrong.

7. Execution Speed and Discipline

Momentum changes everything. When one state reanchors manufacturing, others respond. When a company secures its supply chain, investors reward it. When allies witness America leading with clarity, they align.

Confidence grows through facts on the ground. It rises when workers see plants opening, when investors see returns, and when allies see commitment in action. Every step forward builds conviction.

This is why execution speed matters. The American Sphere must operate at the pace of crisis. Joint task forces meeting with urgency. Data flowing in real time. Decisions made as if survival depends on them.

Because it does.

THE THREE-TO-FIVE-YEAR TIMELINE

Convergence is not permanent protectionism. It is targeted, time-bound action to restore fairness and rebuild resilience.

The logic is simple: Convergence buys time. Tariffs and currency coordination block China from dumping at marginal costs with an undervalued RMB. Without that protection, rebuilding is impossible. New capacity cannot compete against subsidized Chinese exports priced to destroy. With it, the American Sphere can close the gap.

The goal is clear: Reduce dependence on China's supply chains within three to five years. That means:

- **Year One:** Announce a cogent approach. Build confidence. Establish the machinery—Department of Manufacturing and Advanced Technology, war rooms, Treasury and Commerce umbrellas. Begin currency realignment. Start coordinated investments.
- **Years Two–Three:** Scale manufacturing buildout. Diversify supply chains. Enforce technology protection. Deepen allied coordination. Show visible progress—factories opening, jobs created, trade deficits narrowing.
- **Years Four–Five:** Achieve zero trade deficit with China. Complete supply-chain rewiring in critical industries. Lock in currency parity. Solidify the American Sphere as a self-sufficient, trusted economic bloc.

Progress has already begun. Investments are flowing. Tax cuts are in place. And I believe Trump and allied leaders are open to other measures to relieve the pain—price protection, regulatory relief, and more.

Here is the strategic reality: The October 2025 truce in negotiations with China bought us one year. The agreed tariff rollbacks, the committed soybean purchases, the rare earth supply guarantees—these are tactical concessions, not strategic retreats. President Xi agreed to these terms to relieve immediate pressure, but Beijing is betting that Western resolve will weaken before American industrial capacity rebuilds. That the convergence machinery never gets built. That political cycles shift, and this window closes before we act.

The question is what we do with this year. Do we use it to establish a Department of Manufacturing and Advanced Technology, launch pilot production lines, enable reverse choke holds, coordinate allied investments, and demonstrate visible progress in building our own capability? Or do we treat the October truce as a victory and return to business as usual?

This year is not breathing room. It is the starting gun. The Convergence Playbook must be executed with discipline, coordination, and relentless focus.

POLICYMAKERS ALONE CANNOT WIN

Here is the hard truth: Policymakers alone cannot win this fight.

Governments can create the machinery. They can align policies, offer support, and coordinate strategy. But they cannot rebuild industries. They cannot relocate supply chains. They cannot protect technology or innovate at scale.

Only businesses can do that.

You are on the **front line**. Every decision you make—where to invest, where to source, which markets to prioritize—affects the outcome. You have contributed to China's rise. Now you can help break its march.

This is not just Trump's fight. It is not just Washington's problem. It is yours. Your board's. Your investors'. And it requires the same level of courage and clarity that the Convergence Playbook demands from governments.

The next chapter turns to you. How businesses must extricate from China. Where to find growth. How to break free from the choke holds China still controls. And what hard choices you must now make.

Because convergence is not just a government strategy. It is a business imperative. And the companies that move first will shape the future.

Chapter 13

The Business Extrication Playbook

Convergence means one thing: becoming one focused unit against a destructive opponent. In the previous chapter, I laid out the playbook—how governments should coordinate, what machinery they must build, and what support businesses will need.

But here is the reality: Governments create the conditions, the support, the incentives, and the framework that enable businesses to operate in new ways. But governments cannot rebuild industries themselves. They cannot relocate supply chains. They cannot protect technology or innovate at scale.

Only you can do that.

You are on the front line of this economic war. Every decision you make—where to invest, where to source, which markets to prioritize—affects not just your company's future, but the outcome of the broader contest. You have contributed to China's rise, often without realizing it. Now you can help break its march.

This chapter is your playbook. Step by step. Industry by industry. How to extricate from China, where to find growth, what skills and equipment you need, and how to **navigate the pain without letting it become a recession.**

Because this is not a recession path. It is a transformation path. And the companies that move first will define the next era.

WHY NOW

The window for controlled strategic withdrawal is narrowing. The national shift is already underway. President Trump has made reducing the trade deficit with China a core priority. Every month that passes, tariffs rise, supply chains shift, technology controls harden, and China tightens retaliation. Delay will only make the eventual exit more painful and less on your terms.

Washington and Beijing are moving. But what matters more is what you do.

If you sit on a board or lead a company, ask yourself five questions:

1. **Do you have a focused strategy that excludes China?**
2. **Are you transparent about your presence there?**
3. **Have you built a transition plan that can be executed, now?**

4. **Do you have a war room tracking early warning signals of adverse changes ahead?**
5. **Are you communicating with the board and investors with the quality and frequency this moment demands?**

If not, you are vulnerable.

China will keep inviting companies. They will offer facilities, even subsidies. But only while you are useful. And if your product has military or industrial application, that use is short-lived. Once they get what they want, they will cut you off. That is the playbook. It has happened before. It will happen again. Ask Tesla. Ask Micron. Ask GE.

The choice is no longer whether to act. It is when and how. Later in this chapter, I show you the warning signs and how to determine your timing.

FINDING GROWTH BEYOND CHINA

Extricating from China is only half the battle. Once you step out, you must know where to step into. Start now. Do this in parallel. Companies that wait to extricate before finding growth will shrink into defensive shells. Companies that move decisively can seize new frontiers of growth.

Two pillars define this future: the **global south** and the **American Sphere**. Beyond these, as detailed in Chapter 10, lie 180 unaligned countries with $25 trillion in GDP. Most will choose the American Sphere over China's model. Together, they offer the markets, the talent, and the stability to counter China's assault and build a stronger foundation for the next era.

THE GLOBAL SOUTH: THE NEXT FRONTIER

In my 2013 book *Global Tilt*, I wrote that the action would shift below the 34th parallel. Today, that future is here. From Latin America to Africa to Southeast Asia, these economies hold the people, infrastructure needs, and hunger for technology that define the next wave of opportunity.

The numbers tell the story. South Asia is the world's fastest-growing region, expanding at nearly 6 percent annually. India alone is growing between 6.5 and 7 percent—the fastest among the world's largest economies. By 2028, India is expected to overtake Germany to become the world's third-largest economy. By 2030, its GDP is forecast to reach around $7.3 trillion.

At the same time, India is becoming a major global manufacturing and export hub. Apple now produces over $10 billion worth of iPhones in India annually. EV firms are looking to India as a global base. Companies that build in India are not just serving India; they are serving the world.

But India is not alone. Vietnam's economy is expanding at more than 6 percent, Indonesia at about 5 percent. Nigeria, Kenya, and

Ethiopia are emerging as Africa's new industrial anchors. Brazil and Mexico remain Latin America's manufacturing powerhouses. The global pattern is clear: Growth and competitive industry are becoming widely distributed across the global south.

Large economies across the global south will tilt toward the American Sphere. China's debt traps, seized ports, and crushed local industries are creating backlash from Sri Lanka to Zambia to Pakistan. Democracies want to trade with democracies—without the strings attached. The opportunity is mutual: Trade with the American Sphere brings new standards of living and positive trade balances.

But it will not be business as usual. These are not plug-and-play markets. Managers must unlearn what worked in China. Here is what will be required:

- **Capital and staying power.** These economies do not yet offer deep local funding. You must bring the capital and know-how.
- **Different scale logic.** Many markets are smaller. You may need to build regionally—India serving as a hub for multiple geographies.
- **Tailored innovation.** Use AI and local data to adapt products to new needs. Smaller batch sizes. Local assembly.
- **Hands-on leadership.** You cannot delegate these moves. New org structures, business models, local networks, government relations—they all matter.

Done right, the global south offers not just risk mitigation, but real growth.

THE AMERICAN SPHERE: YOUR STABLE BASE

Alongside the search for new markets, companies need a stable base to anchor their expansion. This is where the American Sphere comes in. It is an industrial platform, a network of trusted economies where manufacturing and advanced industrial capacity can be rebuilt at scale. The American Sphere's $60 trillion economy, growing at 3 percent annually with stable currencies, represents **$2 trillion in new market opportunity** every year.

For companies exiting China, this Sphere provides what no single market can offer: secure supply chains, predictable rules, and co-investment opportunities. It is the foundation on which bets on the global south can be made with confidence. A protected base where innovation and production can flourish without CCP interference.

The six powers—the US, the EU, Japan, South Korea, Israel, and the UK—offer complementary strengths: American innovation and capital markets, European industrial depth, Japanese precision manufacturing, Korean electronics and battery technology, Israeli cybersecurity and defense technology, and British financial infrastructure.

And critically, as the previous chapter showed, the convergence framework can provide the umbrella you need: tax incentives, low-cost loans, price protection mechanisms, and regulatory relief.

CHAPTER 13

THE EXTRICATION PROCESS: INDUSTRY BY INDUSTRY

Let me make this concrete. I recently worked with a company that manufactures cellphones and laptops. They came to me asking: How do we reduce dependence on China?

We broke it down. Component by component. What do they need to make? What skills, equipment, and materials are required? What do they have? What do they need to get? Where can they get it?

Here is what we discovered:

What they had:

- Design capability and brand
- Distribution networks
- Customer relationships
- Capital to invest

What they needed:

- Manufacturing capacity outside China
- Supply chain for critical components (processors, displays, batteries, casings)
- Skilled workforce to operate the lines
- Equipment and tooling

Where they could get it:

- **Equipment:** Japan, Germany, and the US all produce precision manufacturing tools
- **Materials:** Diversify sourcing across the American Sphere (Taiwan for chips, South Korea for displays, USA for software)
- **Skills:** Bring in Chinese experts on one-year contracts to train local workers, then phase them out
- **Capital:** Leverage the convergence framework—tax incentives, low-cost loans, regulatory fast-tracking

The plan:

- Year 1: Build pilot line in India or Mexico with transferred Chinese expertise
- Year 2: Scale production, train local workforce, diversify component sourcing
- Year 3: Phase out China dependency entirely, establish regional hubs

The conclusion? **It can be done.** Not overnight. Not without investment. But the path exists.

This is the model for every industry. Break it down. Component by component. Skill by skill. Then build it back, smarter and more resilient.

CHAPTER 13

WHAT THIS COULD LOOK LIKE ACROSS INDUSTRIES

In Chapter 10, we identified that convergence must address the 10 *Made in China 2025* industries plus sectors critical to national security, defense, and raw materials. The same extrication principles apply across all of them. Here we show how it works through six industries that span the full range:

Chemicals:

- We have specialty chemical R&D and advanced formulation capabilities
- What we need: Restore domestic production of base chemicals and polymers gutted by the 90 Percent Model, while expanding capacity in the advanced specialty chemicals (catalysts, precision additives, and high-purity compounds) that China's processing operations require
- Where to get it (examples): Build facilities in the US and Germany, leverage existing European chemical infrastructure, partner with Japan on precision materials

Critical Minerals:

- We have mining resources (USA, Canada, Australia) and processing knowledge
- What we need: Refining facilities, separation technology, magnet production capacity

- Where to get it (examples): MP Materials expanding in the US, Lynas in Australia/Malaysia, Israel for precision extraction technologies, coordinate across the American Sphere for full supply chain

Pharmaceuticals:

- We have the R&D and formulation knowledge
- What we need: API production capacity, fermentation facilities, quality control systems
- Where to get it (examples): Build facilities in the US and India, partner with European chemical suppliers, leverage Israeli biotech innovation

Semiconductors:

- We have design capability (the USA dominates chip design)
- What we need: Fabrication plants, advanced lithography equipment, supply-chain coordination
- Where to get it (examples): TSMC building five US plants, ASML for equipment, Israel for chip design and cybersecurity integration, coordination across the American Sphere

Automobiles/EVs:

- We have brand, design, and assembly knowledge

- What we need: Battery supply chain, electric drivetrains, charging infrastructure
- Where to get it (examples): Build battery plants in the US/Europe, partner with Japan/South Korea on components

Telecom:

- We have network design and equipment manufacturers (Ericsson, Nokia)
- What we need: 5G infrastructure buildout, trusted supply chains, cybersecurity integration
- Where to get it (examples): Partner with European equipment makers, leverage American software capabilities, Israeli cybersecurity integration, coordinate standards across the American Sphere

The pattern is consistent: **We have more than we think. What we need is coordination, capital, and the will to build.**

SHOW THE WORLD WE ARE CATCHING UP

One critical element: demonstrating progress. You do not need to achieve full self-sufficiency overnight. What matters is showing visible momentum.

Set clear milestones:

- **Year 1:** Pilot production and proof of concept

- **Year 2:** 25 percent reduction in China dependence
- **Year 3:** 50 percent reduction
- **Years 4–5:** Full diversification achieved

When investors, governments, and allies see tangible progress—factories opening, jobs created, supply chains functioning—confidence builds. And confidence accelerates investment, which accelerates progress.

This is not about perfection. It is about trajectory. Show you are moving in the right direction, and the ecosystem will support you.

BREAKING THE CHOKE HOLDS

Diversification into new markets is not enough if China still controls the choke points of global industry. Even as companies relocate production and rebuild supply chains, Beijing's grip on critical materials, technologies, and processing systems remains formidable. These choke holds, from rare earths to battery components, are leverage points China can weaponize at any time. Breaking them is a strategic imperative.

The challenge is not just mining or access. It is conversion: turning raw minerals into usable industrial inputs at scale. Today, much of this processing capacity sits in China. Yet China's processing depends on American Sphere inputs it cannot replicate, creating mutual leverage, as the previous chapter detailed. Building alternative processing capacity in the American Sphere will demand coordinated investment, new infrastructure, and updated ESG frameworks. The cost is high. The cost of inaction is higher.

Recent moves show what is possible when urgency meets execution:

- **MP Materials and Lynas** are expanding rare earth refining and magnet production in the US, Australia, and Malaysia to cut dependence on Chinese intermediaries. MP's billion-dollar Texas facility, backed by the Pentagon, will scale output from 1,000 to 10,000 metric tons,[136] supply Apple and GM, and anchor a full domestic supply chain from its California mine to high-grade magnets for EVs, defense, and clean energy.
- **Trump's Defense Production Act order** is accelerating US mining. In March 2025, the Defense Production Act was invoked to fast-track permitting and funding of critical mineral projects for national security.
- **Ukraine has opened its vast critical minerals reserves to the US.** The US now has access to Ukraine's significant deposits of lithium, titanium, and other essential minerals, valued in the trillions.
- **General Motors and Redwood Materials** are building a large-scale battery recycling and cathode production facility in Nevada.[137] The project aims to close the loop on EV supply chains and sharply cut reliance on Chinese battery inputs.

These are early moves, but they set the tone. Breaking the choke holds will require scale, speed, and coordination. Not just nationally, but across the American Sphere. Without it, companies will remain exposed to the very vulnerabilities they are trying to escape.

And here is where your role matters: Demand that your suppliers diversify. Audit your exposure. Build redundancy into critical inputs. Use the convergence umbrella to fund alternative sources. This is not optional. It is survival.

THE BOARDROOM RECKONING

Let me give you one final lens. I have sat in boardrooms. I have seen the shift. One $5 billion company wanted to invest $75 million in China with a state partner. On paper, a solid return. But one director asked the right question: *"Are you creating your own executioner?"* The project was shelved.

Another, a $10 billion firm, wanted to dominate solar in China. But the board asked: *"Are we competing with companies, or with a nation?"* Again, no go.

This is what real leadership looks like. Ask the hard questions. Revisit the assumptions. Plan for a new future.

Seek Truth from Those Already Inside

Speak to CEOs who have tried to leave or are in the process. They will not speak publicly, but they will tell you privately what really happens when China decides you have outlived your usefulness. Ask them:

- When did pricing pressure start?
- When did profitability begin to erode?
- When did the CCP demand more data, training, or tech disclosure?
- When did subsidies stop, replaced by forced capital injections just to survive?

Use their timeline to predict yours. The pattern is consistent. And it is accelerating. What used to take five years now happens in three. If others in your industry faced pressure in year four, you will face it in year three. Plan your exit before the pressure starts.

These stories are real, even if few are told publicly. European governments are already tracking them. Washington should do the same. The transparency will help boards and journalists understand what is really happening. Because this trend is accelerating.

Ask Yourself the Hard Questions

- Is your Chinese competitor growing while your volumes shrink?
- Are they being handed shelf space you cannot access?
- Are they undercutting your price, knowing they will be subsidized to cover the loss?

- Are you being pressured to train their engineers, license your tech, or support their global expansion?

If any of these answers are yes, then the decision has already been made. You are being squeezed out. Your market share is falling. Their capacity is rising. And if their capacity exceeds local demand, you are under the thumb of the 90 Percent Model.

Act with Credibility, or Don't Act at All

Your investors may not like the message. Your board may push back. The analysts may downgrade your stock. That is fine. But your credibility must stay intact. Say what you mean. And deliver what you say.

I have worked with CEOs who have done this right. They faced investor anxiety head-on. They explained the plan. They gave specific downside guidance. They framed the transition as a necessary sacrifice. And when the short-term pain came, they did not blink.

Yes, the stock fell. Yes, some shareholders ran. But those who stayed were the right ones. And post-transition, the business came back stronger. Strategic control returned. And credibility, the rarest currency in leadership, stayed intact.

That is the bar now.

Prepare to Lose the Wrong Investors

Do not soften the message. Do not hedge. Do not delay. Tell the truth early. Lay out the path. Show investors what to expect. Not just the dip, but the destination. Let the fast-money crowd rotate out.

What matters is who stays, whether your team believes, and most of all, whether you execute and follow through.

Build your post-China strategy with specifics: Fund it, set milestones, and stick to them. Because the next board meeting, the next investor call, the next town hall—they will all ask the same question: *What is the plan?*

You cannot afford to bluff.

WHAT YOU NEED TO SUCCEED

When you plan, be brutally honest about what it takes:

Skills:

- Bring in experts, even from China, on limited contracts to train your workforce
- Invest in technical training programs with partners across the American Sphere: Japan for precision manufacturing, Germany for machine tools, the US for automation and AI, Israel for cybersecurity and defense applications, and the UK for industrial design
- Build institutional knowledge that stays with your company

Equipment:

- Source from trusted partners: Germany for machine tools, Japan for precision equipment, and the US for software and automation
- Negotiate as part of the convergence framework (when available) for better pricing and financing

Materials:

- Diversify sourcing across the American Sphere
- Build relationships with alternative suppliers now, before you need them
- Participate in critical minerals initiatives

Capital:

- Leverage the Treasury and Commerce umbrella (when available): tax incentives, low-cost loans, price protection
- Use convergence support (when available) to offset transition costs
- Model the investment over three to five years, not quarterly

Timeline:

- Year 1: Stop new investment in China, build pilot capacity elsewhere

- Years 2–3: Scale production, diversify supply chain, train workforce
- Years 4–5: Complete transition, achieve independence

Pain Points (Be Honest):

- Short-term margin pressure
- Higher input costs during transition
- Potential Chinese retaliation (price wars, market access restrictions)
- Investor anxiety and stock volatility

But this is not a recession: This is an investment in resilience. Companies that complete the transition will have:

- Lower geopolitical risk
- More control over their destiny
- Access to growing markets (global south, American Sphere)
- Government support through the convergence framework
- Long-term competitive advantage

One company, critical to China's goals, ran a 10-year scenario model. They are now exiting in five. Quietly. Safely. On their terms.

BUILD YOUR WAR ROOM

What Washington builds for government, you must build for your company. I urge every major corporation to create its own war room. A physical, virtual, or hybrid space with real-time data, decision logs, and rapid-response playbooks.

Here is what it looks like:

- **A team of analysts** tracking trade disruptions, supply-chain shifts, and capital flows
- **Dashboards powered by AI** that detect global movement in inventory, tariffs, and sanctions
- **Weekly reviews** that assess exposure, reallocate capital, and reroute production

You start defensive: Where are you vulnerable to cash burn, inventory pile-up, port blockages? Then you go offensive: Which suppliers, which markets, which geographies offer better pricing and stability?

The key is response flexibility. Can your system adjust in days? Weeks? Months? The companies that survive will be those that know how to absorb shocks, stay agile, and act with discipline.

Trump is acting at warp speed. He deploys tariffs as tactical weapons—high at first, reduced in negotiation, reimposed on breach. In this term, follow-through is real. No one should assume leniency.

Companies must plan for three cycles at once:

- **Short-term disruption** (logistics, capital costs, investor reaction)
- **Midterm strategy** (new supply chains, local manufacturing)
- **Long-term positioning** (where and how you grow without China)

This is why the playbook must be matched by execution muscle. Execution capacity is now a strategic differentiator.

THE LEADERSHIP MOMENT

The hardest decisions are the ones no one else can make for you. Every board, every CEO, now stands at that edge. The choice is not whether to stay in China a little longer or leave quietly someday. The choice is whether to lead when it matters most.

The companies that will define the next era are those whose leaders face the pain upfront and move with discipline. They will take hits. They will lose investors who were never truly aligned. But they will emerge with control over their future.

This is not a recession path. It is a transformation path. The convergence framework (when executed) will provide the umbrella. The American Sphere can provide the foundation. The global south provides the growth. And you provide the execution.

The window for hesitation is closing. But the window for opportunity is opening. The companies that move first—with clarity, capital, and courage—will not just survive this era. They will lead it.

You have the playbook. You have the support. You have the markets.

Now execute.

To Every Business Leader Caught in the US-China War

You have reached the end of this book. **You now understand the US-China War is not background noise. It is the arena where your business will either thrive or fall.**

The risk is real. Industry after industry has felt the impact. Tariff surges. Frozen inventories. Seized supply chains. Fear of inflation, recession, collapsing valuations. Many executives react like deer in headlights.

Some will not.

Ask yourself: Do you understand what is happening? Do you see the root causes? Do you have a fact-based view of where this is heading?

Can you navigate this alone?

This book gives you clarity. Why China is doing what it is doing. The larger contest at play. And the playbook to act.

The Facts:

- **China's decades-long assault** on American industry and the global order
- **Its 90 Percent Model:** excess production capacity designed to destroy competitors and dominate choke points

- **Its encirclement strategy:** isolating America economically, technologically, militarily
- **Its mission:** to dismantle the American-led world order and replace it with its own

This is deliberate. Strategic. Relentless.

We import goods that we could produce ourselves. But are they really cheap? Or artificially cheap, subsidized to make us stop producing? **That is how 10 industries were gutted.**

Your five-year plans? Obsolete. Your assumptions about stable trade? Broken. **Competitive advantage now depends on how quickly you align with the realities of this contest.**

The war is already on.

Both sides are preparing. Military budgets rising. Economic war capabilities accelerating. In November 2025, Trump announced plans to resume nuclear weapons testing. Xi met with Russia's prime minister to deepen energy, aerospace, and technology investments while Western sanctions tighten. The train line from Moscow to Pyongyang now runs uninterrupted.

These are not distant warnings. They are current moves on the chessboard. Russia-Ukraine, Iran, Indo-Pacific tensions—these are connected, part of a broader strategy to drain American resources and fracture alliances. You cannot wait. **You must plan now, at the same speed as the war planners.**

But this is not inevitable decline. **It is a story of choice.**

America has weapons. **Reverse choke points** China cannot bypass. Taiwan's TSMC, the Netherlands' ASML, US-based Applied Materials—without these three, China cannot build advanced semiconductors. China's rare earth processing depends on specialty chemicals and precision equipment the American Sphere controls. The question is not whether America can win. The question is whether America will coordinate.

I have shown you:

- **The assault:** how China's model works and why it threatens your industry.
- **The vulnerabilities:** where America and its allies are exposed.
- **The playbook:** how convergence can counter China through coordinated action.
- **The business response:** how to extricate, where to find growth, what it takes to rebuild.

The convergence framework I recommend will only work if businesses like yours engage. **Governments can create the machinery. You must execute.**

Now it is on you.

Rethink every dollar going to China. Look for smart exits. Expect friction. Build your post-China strategy with specifics: Fund it, set milestones, stick to them. Communicate clearly with investors. Some will leave. Let them. The ones who stay will build the future with you.

Leverage the opportunities: the global south for growth, the American Sphere for stability, convergence support when it arrives. Build your war room. Track the data. Move with discipline.

The companies that act now, with speed, clarity, and courage, will not just survive this era. They will shape it.

The US-China War is the defining contest of our time. It will reshape industries, alliances, and the global order. **Your company's future depends on which side of this divide you choose and how quickly you act.**

President Xi is playing the long game. **What is yours?**

The silent assault is underway. **Will you be its next casualty, or will you lead the response?**

The choice is yours.

Acknowledgments

This book would not exist without the courage and candor of dozens of business leaders who shared their experiences, insights, and concerns about the deepening economic conflict between the United States and China. Many spoke on condition of anonymity, fearful of commercial or political retaliation. Two CEOs even agreed to co-author this book with me before ultimately withdrawing after discussions with their boards. To all of you who contributed quietly, your honesty and conviction shaped every page of this work. You know who you are, and I am deeply grateful.

Geraldine Willigan, former editor at *Harvard Business Review*, set the foundation. As my longtime collaborator, Geri helped shape the initial draft, establishing the structure and narrative direction and contributing key content throughout. Her editorial instincts and deep understanding of how to communicate complex ideas clearly to senior executives guided this work from beginning to end.

Priyank Nandan brought the depth, precision, and relentless attention to detail this book demanded. His expertise in technology, supply chains, and competitive dynamics—developed over 20 years at Boston Consulting Group, Salesforce, and Accenture across Asia, Europe, and the Americas—was essential to analyzing China's industrial model. He brought quantitative rigor to the analysis, working tirelessly as researcher, analyst, and editor—synthesizing complex economic data, validating claims, challenging assumptions, and sharpening arguments. His dedication and partnership shaped and strengthened this book immensely, from research through to the final manuscript.

Robert Dilenschneider and his team refined my thinking and approach toward the audience. Bob's counsel on how to reach business and policy leaders was invaluable in shaping the book's message and impact.

Mark Fortier also refined my thinking and approach, helping ensure the book's clarity and resonance with its intended readers.

I am greatly indebted to **Rush Doshi** for his guidance through conversation and through his seminal research in *The Long Game: China's Grand Strategy to Displace American Order.* His work on China's long-term strategy deepened my understanding and informed key sections of this book.

John Joyce, my Harvard roommate and friend, was a constant sounding board. His brainstorming, questions, and challenges helped me think through the most difficult arguments in these pages.

I am also grateful to **Rohit Bhargava** and his talented team at Ideapress Publishing for bringing this book to life with professionalism and speed.

ACKNOWLEDGMENTS

My deepest thanks to my office team—**Lisa Laubert, Ajay Kumar, Carol Davis,** and **Cynthia Burr Schumacher**—who supported this project in countless ways and kept everything running while I worked on this book.

Finally, to the CEOs, board members, policymakers, and business leaders I have had the privilege of advising over five decades: Your questions, challenges, and real-world struggles informed every insight in these pages. You taught me to see the world through the eyes of those who must make decisions under uncertainty. This book is my attempt to serve you in return.

—Ram Charan

About the Author

Ram Charan has spent six decades working with CEOs. Not a day goes by that he doesn't speak to a CEO. That's how he learns and tests his ideas for practicality. He works behind the scenes.

The CEO's office is his laboratory. He works with CEOs of small companies and the world's largest corporations across the US, Europe, China, Brazil, Japan, Canada, India, and almost every major industry. He sits on several public and private boards, including some of the most prominent public boards. He understands the CEO mind. He solves the most complex problems CEOs face. Most of his engagements have lasted no less than 10 years. That's how you make an impact.

Dr. Charan is the author of over 36 books. His books are written for practitioners to use. And they use them. *Execution: The Discipline of Getting Things Done* (co-authored with Larry Bossidy) spent 150 weeks on the *New York Times* bestseller list and has sold millions of copies worldwide.

He is a Harvard Business School Baker Scholar with an MBA (High Distinction) and a doctorate in corporate governance. Dr.

Charan taught at Harvard Business School and Northwestern's Kellogg School of Management before launching his consulting practice, where he pioneered a method of decoding strategy from actions rather than slogans and PowerPoint five-year plans.

For more than two decades, Dr. Charan has been forward-looking on China. Over the last five years, he has been actively warning American CEOs about China's direct threat to their businesses. He predicted China's dominance in manufacturing, supply chains, and critical technologies to CEOs and boards years before these dynamics entered mainstream business and policy debate. He has advised over 50 major Chinese companies and served on boards in China, giving him firsthand insight into the strategies detailed in this book.

He was recently recognized with the 2024 Greatest Impact on Corporate Boards Award (*Corporate Board Member*), honored as a "Global Board Legend" at the 2025 Global Corporate Governance Summit (Bombay Stock Exchange), and named to Thinkers50 Coaching Legends 2025.

Dr. Charan is widely regarded as one of the most influential business advisors in the world today.

Read *Fortune* magazine's cover story on Dr. Ram Charan: www.ram-charan.com/story

Endnotes

1 Lewis Jackson, "How China's New Rare Earth Export Controls Work," Reuters, October 10, 2025. https://www.reuters.com/world/china/how-chinas-new-rare-earth-export-controls-work-2025-10-10/.

2 Natalie Sherman, "Trump Threatens to Impose Additional 100% Tariff on China," BBC, October 10, 2025. https://www.bbc.co.uk/news/articles/cn4wkd7729po.

3 Ella Nilsen, René Marsh, and Alayna Treene, "Exclusive: Department of Energy Officials to Meet with White House to Tamp Down Trump's Idea of Explosive Nuclear Testing," CNN, November 14, 2025. https://edition.cnn.com/2025/11/14/politics/nnsa-nuclear-testing-white-house-meeting-exclusive.

4 Nidhi Verma and Florence Tan, "Exclusive: Traders Seek Yuan Payment from Indian State Buyers of Russian Oil, Sources Say," Reuters, October 8, 2025. https://www.reuters.com/business/energy/traders-seek-yuan-payment-indian-state-buyers-russian-oil-sources-say-2025-10-07/.

5 Kanishka Singh and Doina Chiacu, "Trump Again Threatens India with Harsh Tariffs over Russian Oil Purchases," Reuters, August 5, 2025. https://www.reuters.com/world/india/trump-again-threatens-india-with-harsh-tariffs-over-russian-oil-purchases-2025-08-05/.

6 PR Newswire, "Olin Announces Facility Closures," December 11, 2019. https://www.prnewswire.com/news-releases/olin-announces-facility-closures-300972744.html; Kristen Hays, "Olin to Idle 'Significant Portion' of Texas Chlor-Alkali, EDC Capacity," S&P Global, June 14, 2022. https://www.spglobal.com/commodity-insights/en/news-research/latest-news/chemicals/061422-olin-to-idle-significant-portion-of-texas-chlor-alkali-edc-capacity.

7 Henry Edwardes-Evans, "BASF Cuts Ammonia Production in Antwerp, Ludwigshafen on Gas Price," S&P Global, September 27, 2021. https://www.spglobal.com/commodity-insights/en/news-research/latest-news/natural-gas/092721-basf-cuts-ammonia-production-in-antwerp-ludwigshafen-on-gas-price; BASF, "BASF Closes Divestiture of Its Global Pigments Business," June 30, 2021. https://www.basf.com/global/en/media/news-releases/2021/06/p-21-242.

8 Dutch News, "Two Chemicals Plants Shut at Rotterdam Port, Citing High Costs," March 19, 2025. https://www.dutchnews.nl/2025/03/two-chemicals-plants-shut-at-rotterdam-port-citing-high-costs/.

9 Keith Bradsher, "China's Trade Surplus Climbs Past $1 Trillion for First Time," *The New York Times,* December 7, 2025. https://www.nytimes.com/2025/12/07/business/china-trade-surplus.html.

10 "US Economy Posts Strong Second Quarter, Growing at 3% Pace," *The Washington Post,* July 30, 2025. https://www.washingtonpost.com/business/2025/07/30/gdp-q2-economy-tariffs/.

11 Monetary Authority of Singapore and IMF historical exchange rate data, 1971–2025.

12 Authors' analysis based on exchange rate data from International Monetary Fund, People's Bank of China, and World Bank, 1990–2025.

13 John Nash, "The Work of John Nash in Game Theory," Nobel Seminar, December 8, 1994. https://www.nobelprize.org/uploads/2017/05/nash-lecture.pdf.

14 Authors' analysis based on GDP data from World Bank and International Monetary Fund, 2024.

15 Ibid.

16 Ibid.

17 Authors' analysis based on Liberty Ship production data from Smithsonian National Museum of American History.

18 Nupur Anand, "JPMorgan Unveils $1.5 Trillion Plan to Boost Investments in US Strategic Industries," Reuters, October 13, 2025. https://www.reuters.com/business/finance/jpmorgan-unveils-15-trillion-plan-boost-investments-us-strategic-industries-2025-10-13/.

ENDNOTES

19 Authors' analysis based on GDP data from Bureau of Economic Analysis, 2024.

20 The White House, "Establishing the United States Investment Accelerator," March 31, 2025. https://www.whitehouse.gov/presidential-actions/2025/03/establishing-the-united-states-investment-accelerator/.

21 The White House, "Investments," accessed November 2025. https://www.whitehouse.gov/investments/.

22 Reuters, "China's President Xi Meets with Russia's Prime Minister Mishustin," November 4, 2025. https://www.reuters.com/world/china/chinas-president-xi-meets-with-russias-prime-minister-mishustin-2025-11-04/.

23 Authors' analysis based on trade data from US Census Bureau, 2024.

24 Ibid.

25 *The Wall Street Journal*, "What Contributes to the Trade Gap," March 3, 2025, print edition.

26 Authors' analysis based on data from International Monetary Fund, World Bank, and People's Bank of China.

27 Alana Pipe, Drew An-Pham, and Jeanne Whalen, "What to Know About the US Trade Imbalance, in Charts," *The Wall Street Journal,* April 3, 2025. https://www.wsj.com/economy/trade/what-to-know-about-the-u-s-trade-imbalance-in-charts-79b25c0b.

28 Authors' analysis.

29 Authors' analysis based on Center for Strategic and International Studies, *Made in China 2025*, June 2015. https://www.csis.org/analysis/made-china-2025.

30 Authors' analysis based on trade data from World Bank and Statista.

31 Ehsan Soltani, "Mapped: How China Overtook the US in Global Trade (2000–2024)," Visual Capitalist, April 9, 2025. https://www.visualcapitalist.com/cp/how-china-overtook-u-s-in-global-trade-dominance-2000-2024/.

32 Nassos Stylianou, Joe Leahy, William Langley, et al. "Is China's Trade Juggernaut Unstoppable?" *Financial Times,* April 9, 2025. https://ft.pressreader.com/article/281767045050106.

33 *Financial Times*, "The Chinese Goods Americans Most Rely On, from Microwaves to Barbies," April 11, 2025. https://www.ft.com/content/ec96e2ed-5dd6-4c6b-92a0-1b77bf517b36.

34 Goldman Sachs, "Resource Realism: The Geopolitics of Critical Mineral Supply Chains," September 13, 2023. https://www.goldmansachs.com/insights/articles/resource-realism-the-geopolitics-of-critical-mineral-supply-chains; Rico Luman and Ewa Manthey, "China's Export Restrictions on Rare Earths Causes Alarm for Automotive Industry," ING, June 10, 2025. https://think.ing.com/articles/chinas-crackdown-on-rare-earth-causes-alarm-automotive-industry/.

35 Nassos Stylianou, Joe Leahy, William Langley, et al. "Is China's Trade Juggernaut Unstoppable?" *Financial Times,* April 9, 2025. https://ft.pressreader.com/article/281767045050106.

36 Clark Savage, "China Tackles Price Wars as Bloated Solar Sector Amasses Huge Losses," Energy News Beat, September 4, 2025. https://energynewsbeat.co/china-tackles-price-wars-as-bloated-solar-sector-amasses-huge-losses/.

37 DrugPatentWatch, "The Role of China in the Global Generic Drug API Market," September 9, 2025. https://www.drugpatentwatch.com/blog/the-role-of-china-in-the-global-generic-drug-api-market/.

38 The Oregon Group, "78% of US Military Weapon Systems Vulnerable to China's Critical Mineral Dominance," May 1, 2025. https://theoregongroup.com/commodities/rare-earths/78-of-us-military-weapon-systems-potentially-vulnerable-to-china-critical-mineral-dominance/.

39 Robert D. Atkinson, "How Innovative Is China in the Chemicals Industry?" April 15, 2024. https://itif.org/publications/2024/04/15/how-innovative-is-china-in-the-chemicals-industry/.

40 "Vietnam Trade Deal Takes Aim at Backdoor for Chinese Goods," *The Wall Street Journal,* July 3, 2025. https://www.wsj.com/economy/trade/vietnam-trade-deal-takes-aim-at-backdoor-for-chinese-goods-e165a6e7.

41 "Looking Back on Deng Xiaoping's Landmark Visit to Singapore," *The Diplomat*, December 22, 2023. https://thediplomat.com/2023/12/looking-back-on-deng-xiaopings-landmark-visit-to-singapore/.

42 Rush Doshi, *The Long Game: China's Grand Strategy to Displace American Order* (Oxford University Press, 2021).

43 "China Primer: China's Political System," Congressional Research Service, March 1, 2025. https://www.congress.gov/crs-product/IF12505.

44 Charlie Bradley, "China Sends Horror WW3 Threat of Nuclear Strike Hitting in 20 Minutes—'This Is War,'" *Daily Express,* October 8, 2025. https://www.express.co.uk/news/world/2118919/china-sends-horror-ww3-threat.

45 Reuters, "Lula Tells Trump World Does Not Want 'Emperor' After US Threatens BRICS Tariff," July 7, 2025. https://www.reuters.com/world/china/brics-nations-resist-anti-american-label-after-trump-tariff-threat-2025-07-07/.

46 Zeyi Yang, "Why China's Dominance in Commercial Drones Has Become a Global Security Matter," *MIT Technology Review,* June 26, 2024. https://www.technologyreview.com/2024/06/26/1094249/china-commercial-drone-dji-security/.

47 Shanghai Metal Market, "Q1 Global EV Battery Installations: CATL Continues to Lead, Market Share of South Korea's Top Three Battery Makers Shrinks," May 20, 2025. https://www.metal.com/en/newscontent/103335234.

48 Eurasia Rail, "Eurasia Rail Exhibitor Focus: CRRC," June 2025. https://eurasiarail.eu/en/market-insights/eurasia-rail-exhibitor-focus-crrc.

49 Authors' analysis based on multiple sources, including WuXi AppTec, "WuXi AppTec Revenue and Profit Achieved Steady QoQ Growth in 2024," March 17, 2025. https://www.wuxiapptec.com/news/wuxi-news/6025.

50 "How Innovative Is China in the Chemicals Industry?" Information Technology and Innovation Foundation, April 15, 2024. https://itif.org/publications/2024/04/15/how-innovative-is-china-in-the-chemicals-industry/.

51 "Task Force Report No. 83: US Economic Security—Winning the Race for Tomorrow's Technologies," Council on Foreign Relations, October 30, 2025. https://assets.cfr.org/images/TFR83_EconomicSecurity_Full_2025-10-30_Final/TFR83_EconomicSecurity_Full_2025-10-30_Final.pdf.

52 Doris Dokua Sasu, "Share of Chemical Sales Value Worldwide in 2022, by Leading Country or Region," Statista, November 27, 2025. https://www.statista.com/statistics/1247223/global-chemical-sales-market-share-by-country/.

53 Authors' analysis based on multiple sources, including OMR Global (2025), DrugPatentWatch (2025), SME Business Review (2025), Information Technology and Innovation Foundation (2024), FDA registration data, international trade statistics, and company annual reports.

54 BBC, "Former Employee Jailed for 'Raid' on Motorola Secrets," August 30, 2012. https://www.bbc.co.uk/news/business-19419521.

55 Zetta Hannany and Dhika Priambodo, "Huawei Surpasses Nokia in Global Telecom Equipment Market," IDN Financials, September 3, 2025. https://www.idnfinancials.com/news/57029/huawei-surpasses-nokia-in-global-telecom-equipment-market.

56 *Foreign Policy*, "5G Explained: How 5G Networks Will Define Global Power," updated February 23, 2021. https://foreignpolicy.com/2020/01/22/5g-cellular-huawei-china-networks-technology-infrastructure-power-map/.

57 Reuters, "Germany Agrees Phaseout of Huawei, ZTE Components in 5G Core Network," July 11, 2024. https://www.reuters.com/business/media-telecom/germany-agrees-phaseout-huawei-zte-components-5g-core-network-2024-07-11/.

58 MWC Shanghai, "TD Tech Ltd.," accessed December 2025. https://www.mwcshanghai.com/exhibitors/33315-td-tech-ltd.

59 Patrick McGee, *Apple in China* (Scribner, 2025).

60 "The Chinese EV Dilemma: Subsidized yet Striking," Center for Strategic and International Studies, June 20, 2024. https://www.csis.org/blogs/trustee-china-hand/chinese-ev-dilemma-subsidized-yet-striking.

61 Shannon Molloy, "China Executes $347 Billion Plot to Control World's Electric Vehicle Market," News.com.au, July 2, 2024. https://www.news.com.au/technology/motoring/motoring-news/china-executes-347-billion-plot-to-control-worlds-electric-vehicle-market/news-story/5045915379b18598ea0d94f279b3482f.

62 Reuters, "Ford Considers Scrapping F-150 EV Truck, WSJ Reports," November 6, 2025. https://www.reuters.com/business/autos-transportation/ford-considers-scrapping-f-150-ev-truck-wsj-reports-2025-11-06/.

63 Fan Wang, "A New China Tech Visa Has Caught India's Attention—Now Locals Aren't Happy," BBC, October 1, 2025. https://www.bbc.co.uk/news/articles/cvg4eeerzrwo.

64 BBC, "Trump Adds $100,000 Fee for Skilled Worker Visa Applicants," September 19, 2025. https://www.bbc.co.uk/news/articles/cm2zk4l8g26o.

65 Shenzhen Government Online, "New Policies Attract FDI to Shenzhen," March 19, 2025. https://www.sz.gov.cn/en_szgov/news/latest/content/post_12074527.html.

66 "Accelerator State: How China Fosters 'Little Giant' Companies," Mercator Institute for China Studies (MERICS), August 3, 2023. https://merics.org/en/report/accelerator-state-how-china-fosters-little-giant-companies.

67 BWT Beijing, "BWT Plans to Increase Capital by 467 Million Yuan to Accelerate World-Class Technology Independent Innovation," June 22, 2022. https://www.bwt-bj.com/en/content/details24_5429.html.

68 Endovastec, "Endovastec™ Announces Annual Results for 2024: Global Expansion Accelerates as Innovation Drives Quality Development," March 28, 2025. https://www.endovastec.com/428/628.

69 *China Daily*, "WND Company Benefits from Big Investment in R&D," July 11, 2023. https://investinchina.chinadaily.com.cn/s/202307/11/WS64b75513498ea274927c59bb/wnd-company-benefits-from-big-investment-in-r-d.html.

70 *The Economist*, "A Visual Guide to Critical Materials and Rare Earths," March 24, 2025. https://www.economist.com/graphic-detail/2025/03/24/a-visual-guide-to-critical-materials-and-rare-earths; Niccolo Conte, "Charted: America's Import Reliance of Key Minerals," Visual Capitalist, August 4, 2023. https://www.visualcapitalist.com/charted-americas-import-reliance-of-key-minerals/.

71 International Energy Agency, "Global Critical Minerals Outlook 2025," 2025. https://www.iea.org/reports/global-critical-minerals-outlook-2025/overview-of-outlook-for-key-minerals.

72 Daniel Ramos, "Bolivia Says China's CBC to Invest $1 Billion in Lithium Plants," Reuters, November 26, 2024. https://www.reuters.com/markets/commodities/bolivia-says-chinas-cbc-invest-1-billion-lithium-plants-2024-11-26/.

73 Select Committee on the CCP, "REPORT: American Financial Institutions Funneled Billions into PRC Companies Fueling the CCP's Military, Surveillance State, and Uyghur Genocide," April 18, 2024. https://democrats-selectcommitteeontheccp.house.gov/media/press-releases/report-american-financial-institutions-funneled-billions-prc-companies-fueling.

74 Christoph Nedopil Wang, "China Belt and Road Initiative (BRI) Investment Report 2025 H1," Green Finance & Development Center, July 17, 2025. https://greenfdc.org/china-belt-and-road-initiative-bri-investment-report-2025-h1/.

75 "Chinese Ships Are Carrying America's Cargo. The US Wants to Reverse That." *The Wall Street Journal*, March 14, 2025. https://www.wsj.com/world/china/china-cargo-ship-trump-shipbuilding-823b1c9c.

76 Peter Martin, Ben Westcott, Viktoria Dendrinou, et al. "China's Global Network of Shipping Ports Is Too Big for Trump to Unravel," *Bloomberg,* October 20, 2025. https://www.bloomberg.com/graphics/2025-china-ports/.

77 Reuters, "Xi Jinping Opens Huge Port in Peru Funded by China," NBC News, November 15, 2024. https://www.nbcnews.com/news/world/xi-jinping-opens-huge-port-peru-funded-china-rcna180289.

78 "The Game of Loans: How China Bought Hambantota," Center for Strategic and International Studies, April 2, 2018. https://www.csis.org/analysis/game-loans-how-china-bought-hambantota.

79 David Rogers, "Nicaragua Revives Interoceanic Canal as Trump Eyes Panama," *Global Construction Review,* January 24, 2025. https://www.globalconstructionreview.com/nicaragua-revives-interoceanic-canal-as-trump-eyes-panama/#:~:text=David%20Rogers,Lake%20Xolotl%C3%A1n%2C%20north%20of%20Managua.

80 Sean Lyngaas, "Congressional Probe Finds Communications Gear in Chinese Cranes, Raising Spying Concerns," CNN, March 8, 2024. https://edition.cnn.com/2024/03/07/politics/congressional-probe-communications-gear-chinese-cranes.

81 US-China Economic and Security Review Commission, "Hearing on China's Stockpiling and Mobilization Measures for Competition

and Conflict," June 13, 2024. https://www.uscc.gov/sites/default/files/2024-06/June_13_2024_Hearing_Transcript.pdf.

82 Congressional Research Service, "Undersea Telecommunication Cables: Technology Overview and Issues for Congress," September 13, 2022. https://www.congress.gov/crs_external_products/R/HTML/R47237.html; Jared Cohen, "The AI Economy's Massive Vulnerability," *Foreign Policy*, February 20, 2025. https://foreignpolicy.com/2025/02/20/ai-economy-undersea-cables-international-data-infrastructure/.

83 "Safeguarding Subsea Cables: Protecting Cyber Infrastructure amid Great Power Competition," Center for Strategic and International Studies, August 16, 2024. https://www.csis.org/analysis/safeguarding-subsea-cables-protecting-cyber-infrastructure-amid-great-power-competition.

84 Kieran Kelly, "Chinese Vessel 'Sabotaged' Baltic Deep Sea Cables and May Have Been Under Orders from Russia," *The Telegraph,* November 27, 2024. https://www.telegraph.co.uk/world-news/2024/11/27/chinese-vessel-sabotaged-baltic-deep-sea-cables-russia/.

85 Yimou Lee and Ben Blanchard, "In a First, Taiwan Charges Chinese Ship Captain with Damaging Undersea Cables," Reuters, April 11, 2025. https://www.reuters.com/world/asia-pacific/first-taiwan-charges-chinese-ship-captain-with-damaging-undersea-cables-2025-04-11/.

86 Thomas Barrabi, "Google, Meta Warned That Undersea Internet Cables at Risk for Chinese Espionage," *New York Post,* May 20, 2024. https://nypost.com/2024/05/20/business/google-meta-warned-that-undersea-internet-cables-at-risk-for-chinese-espionage-report/.

87 Erin L. Murphy and Matt Pearl, "China's Underwater Power Play: The PRC's New Subsea Cable-Cutting Ship Spooks International Security Experts," Center for Strategic and International Studies, April 4, 2025. https://www.csis.org/analysis/chinas-underwater-power-play-prcs-new-subsea-cable-cutting-ship-spooks-international.

88 US-China Economic and Security Review Commission, "2024 Report to Congress," November 2024. https://www.uscc.gov/sites/default/files/2024-11/2024_Annual_Report_to_Congress.pdf.

89 Sebastian Horn, Carmen M. Reinhart, and Christoph Trebesch, "China's Overseas Lending," IMF 20th Annual Research Conference, July 3, 2019. https://www.imf.org/-/media/files/conferences/2019/20th-annual-research-conference/session1-horn-reinhart-trebesch.pdf.

90 Observatory of Economic Complexity (OEC), "China Country Profile," data through October 2025. https://oec.world/en/profile/country/chn.

91 Aaron Ross and Karin Strohecker, "Exclusive: Congo Reviewing $6 Bln Mining Deal with Chinese Investors—Finmin," Reuters, August 27, 2021. https://www.reuters.com/world/africa/exclusive-congo-reviewing-6-bln-mining-deal-with-chinese-investors-finmin-2021-08-27/.

92 Rachel Savage, "China's Waiver of African Interest-Free Loans Worth 1% or Less of Its Lending to Continent," Reuters, September 12, 2022. https://www.reuters.com/world/china/chinas-waiver-african-interest-free-loans-worth-1-or-less-its-lending-continent-2022-09-12/; Yahoo Finance, "China Writes Off More Interest-Free Loans to Africa, But Is the Move Just Symbolic?" September 10, 2024. https://finance.yahoo.com/news/china-writes-off-more-interest-093000605.html.

93 "How China Capitalized on US Indifference in Latin America," *The Wall Street Journal*, November 14, 2024. https://www.wsj.com/world/china-xi-jinping-latin-america-acf6dbc1.

94 Craig Singleton, "Mapping the Expansion of China's Global Military Footprint," Foundation for Defense of Democracies, last updated April 30, 2024. https://www.fdd.org/plaexpansion/.

95 Mia Jankowicz, "North Korea's Intercontinental Ballistic Missiles Could Hit Central US in Just 33 Minutes, Says Chinese Study," *Business Insider,* March 2023. https://www.businessinsider.com/north-korea-icbm-hit-usa-33-minutes-china-study-says-2023-3.

96 *Financial Times*, "China Is on a Mission to Ensure Its Food Security," September 1, 2022. https://www.ft.com/content/363c94c1-afed-49b3-aa09-
f31227819791.

97 "Pentagon Officials Provide Data on Unsafe Chinese Fighter Intercepts over Western Pacific," US Naval Institute News, October 17, 2023. https://news.usni.org/2023/10/17/pentagon-officials-provide-data-on-unsafe-chinese-fighter-intercepts-over-western-pacific.

98 US Department of Defense, "Senior Defense Official Briefs on 2024 China Military Power Report," December 18, 2024. https://www.defense.gov/News/Transcripts/Transcript/Article/4009708/senior-defense-official-briefs-on-2024-china-military-power-report/.

99 US Department of Defense, "Military and Security Developments Involving the People's Republic of China 2024," December 18, 2024. https://media.defense.gov/2024/Dec/18/2003615520/-1/-1/0/MILITARY-AND-SECURITY-DEVELOPMENTS-INVOLVING-THE-PEOPLES-REPUBLIC-OF-CHINA-2024.PDF; US Department of Defense, "Department of Defense Releases the President's Fiscal Year 2025 Defense Budget," March 11, 2024. https://www.defense.gov/News/Releases/Release/Article/3703410/department-of-defense-releases-the-presidents-fiscal-year-2025-defense-budget/.

100 "China Naval Modernization: Implications for US Navy Capabilities—Background and Issues for Congress," Congressional Research Service, April 24, 2025. https://www.congress.gov/crs-product/RL33153.

101 Center for Strategic and International Studies, "Looking South: A Conversation with Gen. Laura Richardson on Security Challenges in Latin America," August 4, 2023. https://www.csis.org/analysis/looking-south-conversation-gen-laura-richardson-security-challenges-latin-america.

102 Mark Milley and Eric Schmidt, "Is America Ready for the Wars of the Future?" *Foreign Affairs*, October 2024. https://www.foreignaffairs.com/united-states/ai-america-ready-wars-future-ukraine-israel-mark-milley-eric-schmidt.

103 Globe Newswire, "Connected Commercial Drones Report 2025: Asia-Pacific Leads in Drone Adoption with DJI Holding a Dominant 70% Global Market Share," April 8, 2025. https://www.globenewswire.com/fr/news-release/2025/04/08/3057358/0/en/Connected-Commercial-Drones-Report-2025-Asia-Pacific-Leads-in-Drone-Adoption-with-DJI-Holding-a-Dominant-70-Global-Market-Share.html.

104 James Pomfret and Jessie Pang, "Chinese Researchers Develop AI Model for Military Use on Back of Meta's Llama," Reuters, November 1, 2024. https://www.reuters.com/technology/artificial-intelligence/chinese-researchers-develop-ai-model-military-use-back-metas-llama-2024-11-01/.

105 Bojan Stojkovski, "China's PLA Uses DeepSeek AI in Non-Combat Roles, Battlefield Deployment Possible," Interesting Engineering, March 23, 2025. https://interestingengineering.com/military/china-pla-deepseek-ai-non-combat-operations.

106 Hepeng Jia, "China's Plan to Recruit Talented Researchers," *Nature,* January 17, 2018. https://www.nature.com/articles/d41586-018-00538-z.

107 "Here's How Much Aid the United States Has Sent Ukraine," Council on Foreign Relations, July 15, 2025. https://www.cfr.org/article/how-much-us-aid-going-ukraine.

108 Brenda Goh, "China Says It May Speed Up Rare Earths Application Approvals for EU," Reuters, June 7, 2025. https://www.reuters.com/world/china/china-says-it-may-speed-up-rare-earths-application-approvals-eu-2025-06-07/.

109 Sam Boocker and David Wessel, "The Changing Role of the US Dollar," Brookings Institution, August 23, 2024. https://www.brookings.edu/articles/the-changing-role-of-the-us-dollar/.

110 Manuela Andreoni and Lisandra Paraguassu, "BRICS Nations Resist 'Anti-American' Label After Trump Tariff Threat," Reuters, July 7, 2025. https://www.reuters.com/world/china/brics-nations-resist-anti-american-label-after-trump-tariff-threat-2025-07-07/.

111 Paul Mackel, Joey Chew, and Jingyang Chen, "RMB—Internationalisation Is Not Over," Central Banking, April 15, 2024. https://www.centralbanking.com/hsbc-reserve-management-trends-2024/7960672/rmb-internationalisation-is-not-over; Asia House, "The Renminbi's Rise and Its Accelerated Use in Global Trade Finance," May 21, 2023. https://www.asiahouse.org/2023/05/21/the-renminbis-rise-and-its-accelerated-use-in-global-trade-finance/; People's Bank of China, "RMB Internationalization Report," 2023. https://www.pbc.gov.cn/en/3688241/3688636/3828468/4756463/5163932/2023120819545781941.pdf.

112 Weizhen Tan, "China Restricted Imports from Australia. Now Australia Is Selling Elsewhere," CNBC, June 2, 2021. https://www.cnbc.com/2021/06/03/australia-finds-new-markets-for-coal-barley-amid-china-trade-fight.html.

113 Ellen M. Burstein and Camille G. Caldera, "Harvard Took in $1.1 Billion from 63 Nations from 2013–2019, per Department of Education," *The*

Harvard Crimson, February 13, 2020. https://www.thecrimson.com/article/2020/2/13/harvard-billion-foreign-funds/.

114 Lingling Wei, "Xi Has Spent Decades Preparing for a Cold War with the US," *The Wall Street Journal,* July 4, 2025. https://www.wsj.com/world/china/china-xi-us-cold-war-trade-strategy-81d0eda1.

115 Council on Foreign Relations, "China Standards 2035 and the Plan for World Domination—Don't Believe China's Hype," June 3, 2020. https://www.cfr.org/blog/china-standards-2035-and-plan-world-domination-dont-believe-chinas-hype.

116 "False Promises II: Continuing Gap Between China's WTO Commitments and Its Practices," Information Technology and Innovation Foundation (ITIF), July 26, 2021. https://itif.org/publications/2021/07/26/false-promises-ii-continuing-gap-between-chinas-wto-commitments-and-its/.

117 Alexander Conner and David Wessel, "What Is the Status of Russia's Frozen Sovereign Assets?" Brookings Institute, June 24, 2025. https://www.brookings.edu/articles/what-is-the-status-of-russias-frozen-sovereign-assets/.

118 Author's analysis; US Department of Energy, "National Laboratories." https://www.energy.gov/national-laboratories; MITRE, "FFRDCs: A Primer." https://www.mitre.org/news-insights/publication/ffrdcs-primer.

119 American Immigration Council, "New American Fortune 500," 2023. https://www.americanimmigrationcouncil.org/research/new-american-fortune-
500-2023.

120 The Select Committee on the CCP, "COMMITTEE REPORT: American VC Firms Investing Billions into PRC Companies Fueling the CCP's Military, Surveillance State, and Uyghur Genocide," February 8, 2024. https://selectcommitteeontheccp.house.gov/media/press-releases/committee-report-american-vc-firms-investing-billions-prc-companies-fueling.

121 BBC News, "See the Trump Tariffs List by Country," updated August 7, 2025. https://www.bbc.co.uk/news/articles/c5ypxnnyg7jo.

122 Felix Richter, "US Tariff Revenue Surges amid Trump's Trade War," Statista, July 28, 2025. https://www.statista.com/chart/34892/us-government-receipts-from-customs-duties/.

123 The White House, "Investing in America." https://www.whitehouse.gov/investments/.

124 *Financial Times*, "Trump Wants 5% NATO Defence Spending Target, Europe Told," December 20, 2024. https://www.ft.com/content/35f490c5-3abb-4ac9-8fa3-65e804dd158f.

125 The White House, "Fiscal Year 2026 Discretionary Budget Request," May 2025. https://www.whitehouse.gov/wp-content/uploads/2025/05/Fiscal-Year-2026-Discretionary-Budget-Request.pdf.

126 "Tariff Impacts: US Companies Cut Investments in China to Record Lows," World Economic Forum, July 30, 2025. https://www.weforum.org/stories/2025/07/tariff-impacts-us-companies-cut-investments-china-record-lows/.

127 American Chamber of Commerce in China (AmCham China), "Global Media Responds to the 2025 China Business Climate Survey," February 14, 2025. https://www.amchamchina.org/global-media-responds-to-the-2025-china-business-climate-survey/.

128 Katharina Buchholz, "Higher Tariffs Here to Stay Despite Trade War De-Escalation?" Statista, May 13, 2025. https://www.statista.com/chart/34447/additional-tariffs-by-the-us-on-china-and-vice-versa-2025/.

129 *The Economic Times*, "Apple's iPhone Production Touches $10 Billion Production Mark in India, Courtesy PLI," November 25, 2024. https://economictimes.indiatimes.com/industry/cons-products/electronics/apples-iphone-production-touches-10-bn-production-mark-in-india-courtesy-pli/articleshow/115654735.cms.

130 Osmond Chia, "Starbucks to Sell Majority Stake in China Business," BBC News, November 2025. https://www.bbc.co.uk/news/articles/cn0g90376j5o.

131 East & Partners, "1 in 2 Corporates Plan to Reshore Supply Chain Away from China," September 27, 2024. https://eastandpartners.com/news/1-in-2-corporates-plan-to-reshore-supply-chain-away-from-china-gtr/.

132 Chris Isidore, "US Firm Agrees to Buy Panama Canal Ports at Center of Trump Fury," CNN, March 5, 2025. https://edition.cnn.com/2025/03/04/business/panama-canal-port-deal-trump.

133 Author's analysis and field visit.

134 Author's analysis based on multiple sources, both primary and secondary.

135 Clariant, "Clariant Celebrates Care Chemicals Expansion at Daya Bay, Strengthening Its Position in China," November 5, 2025. https://www.clariant.com/en/Corporate/News/2025/11/Clariant-celebrates-Care-Chemicals-expansion-at-Daya-Bay-strengthening-its-position-in-China.

136 MP Materials, "MP Materials Announces Transformational Public-Private Partnership with the Department of Defense to Accelerate US Rare Earth Magnet Independence," July 10, 2025. https://investors.mpmaterials.com/investor-news/news-details/2025/MP-Materials-Announces-Transformational-Public-Private-Partnership-with-the-Department-of-Defense-to-Accelerate-U-S-Rare-Earth-Magnet-Independence/default.aspx.

137 General Motors, "GM and Redwood Materials Pursue Use of US-Built Batteries for Energy Storage," July 16, 2025. https://news.gm.com/home.detail.html/Pages/news/us/en/2025/jul/0716-GM-Redwood-Materials-pursue-use-US-built-batteries-energy-storage.html.